What can we do to sto
and even in the church.
wisdom, stories and truth, Kevin Glenn invites his readers to follow Christ in
a movement toward compassionate civility that will yield spiritual, emotional
and relational rewards for those who accept his invitation.

- Dr. David T. Lamb,
Associate professor of Old Testament, Biblical Seminary
Author of *God Behaving Badly*

Civil disagreement and even debate, when done in the spirit of Christ, are
healthy and helpful. But when disagreements descend into second-guessing
motives, distortions of one another's words, mischaracterizations of one
another's views, and personal attacks, then we've moved into the flesh. The
net is that the name of Jesus gets tarnished in no small way. So how do we
change that? Kevin's book contributes to this question with elegance, grace,
and humor. And I'm glad it exists.

- Frank Viola
Blogger, Speaker, Author of *Jesus Now, Revise Us Again, Beyond Evangelical*,
frankviola.com

Kevin Glenn's *Hand Over Fist* offers hope to those in the front-lines of the
Christian faith that an open-handed generosity of spirit and gentle civility
can turn conflicts of interest into communities of imagination and integrity.

- Lori Wagner
Pastor, Poet, Co-Author of *The Seraph Seal*

Hand Over Fist presents us with on-the-ground, everyday practices of "critical
thinking" that make true criticism a form of cheer-leading and civility. Here
is a book that shows how, when criticism lashes out at you, red in tooth and
claw, you can keep it red, but red in forgiveness and compassion.

- Dr. Leonard Sweet
E. Stanley Jones Professor of Evangelism – Drew University, Distinguished
Visiting Professor – George Fox University, Semiotician, Author of *The Well
Played Life, Giving Blood*, and co-author of *Jesus: A Theography*

Hand Over Fist

An Invitation to Christ-Centered Civility

KEVIN D. GLENN

WESTBOW
PRESS
A DIVISION OF THOMAS NELSON
& ZONDERVAN

All scripture quotations, unless otherwise indicated, are taken from the Holy
Bible, New International Version®, NIV®. Copyright ©1973, 1978, 1984, 2011 by
Biblica, Inc.™ Used by permission of Zondervan. All rights reserved worldwide._
www.zondervan.com The "NIV" and "New International Version" are trademarks
registered in the United States Patent and Trademark Office by Biblica, Inc.™

WestBow Press books may be ordered through booksellers or by contacting:

WestBow Press
A Division of Thomas Nelson & Zondervan
1663 Liberty Drive
Bloomington, IN 47403
www.westbowpress.com
1 (866) 928-1240

Because of the dynamic nature of the Internet, any web addresses or
links contained in this book may have changed since publication and
may no longer be valid. The views expressed in this work are solely those
of the author and do not necessarily reflect the views of the publisher,
and the publisher hereby disclaims any responsibility for them.

Any people depicted in stock imagery provided by Thinkstock are models,
and such images are being used for illustrative purposes only.
Certain stock imagery © Thinkstock.

ISBN: 978-1-4908-4021-5 (sc)
ISBN: 978-1-4908-4022-2 (hc)
ISBN: 978-1-4908-4020-8 (e)

Library of Congress Control Number: 2014910560

Printed in the United States of America.

WestBow Press rev. date: 7/3/2014

To my wife, Serena,

my daughter, Emily, and

my son, Cameron

To my Grandmother,

Cora Lee Hutchison

CONTENTS

FOREWORD

Children are not born with good manners. Children are not characterized by congenital civility. One of the most common injuries in toddler day-care centers is of children being bitten by other children. Reinhold Niebuhr, one of the great theologians of the 20th century, confessed that an infant, no matter how cute, was infallible proof of the doctrine of original sin.

It takes years of patience and endurance and constant care to teach toddlers that instead of snarling and snapping over their crackers and crayons, they should share. It is a hard lesson to learn. But it is the first crucial step necessary to create compassionate human beings out of competitive creatures. And it is a lesson we never can stop learning throughout the length of our lives.

For some reason, it appears that Christians need to learn this lesson more than anyone. Already in the late second century the pagan Celsus observed that though Jews and Christians quarreled, they did not quarrel as loudly and viciously as different groups of Christians quarreled with each other. Too much of Christianity has become a razor-bladed religion which doesn't have critics, only crusaders. Roland Bainton, the great Reformation scholar of another era, said that the crusader spirit had four premises: 1) the cause is holy; 2) the crusaders are godly, the enemy is ungodly; 3) God fights for the crusaders and against their opponents; 4) the war is prosecuted unsparingly with a take-no-prisoners mentality.

Sound like any place you know?

Kevin Glenn's *Hand Over Fist: An Invitation to Christ-Centered Civility* is critical of the church's pervasive culture of criticism. In the best tradition of literary critics, who are supposed to tell us what is good, what is interesting, what is valuable, what is lasting--giving true "criticism" a positive not negative underlying thrust--Glenn presents us with on-the-ground, everyday practices of "critical thinking" that make true criticism a form of cheer-leading and civility. Here is a book that shows how, when criticism lashes out at you, red in tooth and claw, you can keep it red, but red in forgiveness and compassion.

After the death of Nelson Mandela (1918-2013), there were those who wondered what more might have been accomplished had he not been imprisoned for those twenty seven years by his government. If ever anyone in the past one hundred years epitomized civility under fire, it was Nelson Mandela. Yet it was his experience of imprisonment, his long steeping in suffering, which ultimately enabled him to extend a hand of reconciliation instead of retaliation to those who had imprisoned him and oppressed his nation. What Mandela lived and breathed "when no one was watching" is what made it possible for him to become the world-shaping leader of a nation when everyone was watching.

Hand Over Fist is full of actions to take, stands to make, convictions to put at stake that no one else may ever see or notice, but which will make the most impact over the course of time. Every unheralded, un-recorded act of civility adds a dab of mortar, swoosh of cement, to the foundational structures and sacrificial behaviors which enable humanity to stand taller than itself—-and for Christians to fight fair with each other.

Dr. Leonard Sweet
E. Stanley Jones Professor of Evangelism: Drew University, Madison, New Jersey Visiting Distinguished Professor: George Fox University, Portland, Oregon.

ACKNOWLEDGEMENTS

I remember first trying to explain the idea for this book to Phil Newell, my doctoral advisor. To say it was a meandering ramble-fest would be an understatement. Phil listened patiently, and let me ramble. He's done that a lot over the past few years, but he began asking questions: the kind of questions that communicated to me from the start that he believed there was substance to the scattered ideas. Phil kept asking questions that drew out what I didn't even know was there. If any good comes of this effort, it is Phil Newell who deserves credit for never letting me stop talking.

My doctoral cohort, and the staff and faculty at George Fox University have become a family. They never ceased to be an encouraging voice and motivator. Cliff Berger, thank you for your constant guidance with my many questions and for your helpful motivation. Loren Kerns, you chiseled away at an undefined topic like a skilled artist. It was uncomfortable, it hurt, it was frustrating, it made me angry; and it made me better. I'm glad you did it.

Dr. Richard Carlson, Marie Knowles, and Kellie Moore, thank you for your wise and helpful edits, suggestions, and genuine support.

To my wife, Serena, and my children, Cameron and Emily. You exhibited the definition of patience, encouragement, and accountability. You kept me honest as a husband and dad, kept me motivated as a student, and kept me laughing the whole time.

To my mentor, Leonard Sweet, you've impacted my thinking and spiritual journey more than you realize. I'll never look at a tire swing the same way.

INTRODUCTION

As a pastor and writer, I am in constant conversation with a wide variety of beliefs in and around the scope of Christianity. I often find myself playing referee between Christians, while unbelievers look on in bewilderment at the stark contrast between our message of grace and our family feuds. Lifelong church involvement and 23 years of church ministry have given me a front row seat to the diminishing civility that has come to define the way in which Christians discuss controversial issues. It is no surprise we seem to be known more for our internal battles than for a united message of grace. We can and must do better. While many resources define and defend our beliefs, there exists a need to directly address the growing problem of incivility among Christian brothers and sisters when those beliefs differ.

We need a hand.

We need the humility to open our hands and ask for help, the boldness to lift up our hand to incivility and say, "enough," and the confidence to hold out our hand to offer help and guidance to others. That's hard to do with a clenched fist. This book is an appeal to the church to unclench our fists, open our hands, and help address the problem of incivility.

Sounds good, right? If we were face to face, you might offer your open palm for a high five, and I would take you up on it. But what's next? We need context; a first-hand account of the problem. That's where we'll begin. You'll see just how pervasive incivility is in our culture, and sadly, how the church often looks no different.

Then we'll examine the ways people from various disciplines and points of interest are seeking to get a handle on this problem, gaining valuable insight from the worlds of conflict resolution, communication, business, family systems theory, and even my daughter's eyeball.

In addition, I am very excited to introduce you to a couple of principles that I believe are two of the best kept secrets followers of Jesus can apply toward a civility grounded in conviction and compassion. One involves learning how to listen and look for the story behind the words we use when we communicate. There's often more happening behind the words than the words themselves could ever convey.

The other will help us see how the best solution to some problems is no "solution" at all. Instead, the best and maybe the only way forward is to manage the tension created by two sides that oppose each other, but need each other (kind of like my marriage, but that's another book).

The primary goal of this book is to provide the Christian community with tools to recognize various forms of conflict, interpret those conflicts appropriately, and engage those conflicts through a conversational process that equips and empowers Christians to participate in civil discourse. To that end, this book explores *why* civility is important and *how* Christians can approach conversations in manner that facilitates unity within the Body of Christ, and improved witness to the world.

And the solution to all of it, is in the palm of your hand. Now how 'bout that high five? Let's get started!

Kevin D. Glenn
Orcas Island, Washington
18 March, 2014

CHAPTER 1

Whatever Happened to Just Being Civil?

*Be civil to all, sociable to many, familiar with
few, friend to one, enemy to none.*
—*Ben Franklin*

*When once the forms of civility are violated, there
remains little hope of return to kindness or decency.*
—*Samuel Johnson*

Several years ago, I was driving to dinner with my wife. It was a
beautiful Florida evening, and we were anticipating the tranquility of
a good meal while the sun slipped below the horizon. My focus was
broken when I saw a man spring from his car. He began screaming
at the driver behind him and pounding his fist on the hood of
that driver's car. Other drivers began to honk, since the incident
was blocking traffic, but the screaming man continued to stand in
front of the offender's car. To my shock, the driver hit the gas and
sent the screaming man tumbling onto his hood and then onto
the pavement. With the screaming man on the ground, the driver
attempted to go on his way.

I pulled into a gas station and called 9-1-1. I'll never forget the
feeling of reporting to the dispatcher what I saw. She repeated, "He
actually hit the other person on purpose?" Officers were dispatched,
and I went to check on the man who was hit. He was still screaming

curses but was on the ground holding his knee. I helped him to the parking lot. Other witnesses had used their cars to prevent the other person from driving away. It was a chaotic scene. Several of us had to keep the men separated while police were en route. Little could be done to control their verbal salvos, which only grew worse as the wives of each man joined the fray. An ambulance carried away the screaming man (his screams decreased as the sedatives took effect), while the other driver was taken away in handcuffs by a police cruiser. Police questioned other witnesses and me about what we saw.

As the officers departed, several of us who had witnessed the ordeal gathered in the gas station parking lot and simply looked at each other in disbelief. We had just witnessed a shocking display of utter disregard for the dignity, respect, safety, and concern due to another person and to the common good of the community. The actions of these two men not only affected their personal lives, but the lives of each of us involved who had been impacted by what we had just experienced. An elderly gentleman raised both hands in the air, shook his head, and asked, "Did we really just see all that? What on earth is wrong with people? Whatever happened to just being civil?"

The image of that gentleman's posture is forever imprinted on my memory. It was a posture of confusion, disbelief, and helplessness. His raised hands resembled the "stick-'em up" posture of someone surrendering to an aggressor. What ever happened to just being *civil*?

Civil? What did that mean? It was the first time in my life that I had actually listened to that particular word. I had surely heard it spoken before, but this event planted the word into my consciousness like a seed. It began to take root, and, like an aggressive vine, has sprung forth throughout the variety of situations, conversations, and interactions we encounter in daily living. The incident created in me a heightened sensitivity to my own interactions with friends, family, parishioners, strangers, critics, and all others the Scriptures might include in the category of "neighbor". Not only was I troubled by the uncivil thoughts and actions I entertained when faced with conflict, but I began to notice just how little I encountered civility, respect, and simple courtesy in day-to-day life.

Just look around, and you can understand why that man threw up his hands in helpless resignation. Our culture rewards incivility. Television shows that feature vocal and physical aggression between self-absorbed housewives, raging radio talk show hosts, and opposing political pundits; and a news media that lives by the rule, "If it bleeds, it leads," provide a consistent intake of incivility, making it a normalized form of expression. Look at the blogosphere, with its trolls, sock puppets, and other cyber-culprits spewing hateful rhetoric. Facebook threads and Twitter feeds feature rudeness that goes viral. In the flood and fray, we throw up our hands and ask, "What happened?"

What gets rewarded gets repeated, retweeted, renewed for another season on TV, replayed online, and reinforced by a culture that just can't get enough. Yet it seems we've had enough. Indeed, from one's bedroom at home to one's break room at work, civility is something we desire from others but a quality we have trouble expressing toward others, especially if we disagree with them.

But there's another way to interpret the posture of the gentleman in the story. The helplessness and resignation may certainly be a posture of our culture. In fact, I argue that our culture has a love/hate relationship with incivility. It's entertaining to watch on reality TV, but in reality, it's a problem we're really tired of. Civility is desired and called for by a culture that rejects absolute standards of morality and enjoys being entertained by the very thing it wants to see diminished. How's that working? According to the research for this book: not so well.

Calls for civility from a relativistic culture to a relativistic culture are about as compelling as the brilliant parenting tips I confidently used to give back when I had no children of my own. Those parents politely smiled, nodded, and thought, "Great theories; talk to me when you have something solid." (If you are one of those parents and are reading this, please accept my apology.)

3

I can see the gentleman's posture as one of sacred surrender, an act of prayer, and a stance of humble readiness to receive something better. His face is looking up, as if looking for a solution, his arms wide, willing to receive direction, his hands open and ready to take and to share what comes as a solution. The image for me has become a posture of worship, where followers of Jesus open their hearts and hands to the strength of our diverse unity and become the community that embodies the very civility our society is searching for.

What Is Civility?

There are diverse approaches to defining civility. Some choose to describe what civil behavior looks like as opposed to how someone might define the word itself. Based on the belief that "the world could be a bit more polite, a bit kinder, and a bit friendlier," John Sweeney and his colleagues at the Brave New Workshop Comedy Theatre collaborated to produce *Return to Civility: A Speed of Laughter Project.* The work contains three hundred and sixty-five very down-to-earth, common-courtesy suggestions to help create a more civilized world, in an attempt to "reclaim the appreciation once displayed for our fellow human beings, our selves, and our planet."

Motivated by his experience at a concert during which a Grammy award-winning musician stopped her set to ask the audience to quiet down, Sweeney inspired his fellow comedians to think of daily suggestions for one to lead a more considerate and considered life. According to Sweeney, the suggestions are not focused on changing others, "but rather, are a list of ways we can alter our own actions and behaviors."[1]

In contrast, Sara Hacala, protocol consultant and author of *Saving Civility: 52 Ways to Tame Rude, Crude & Attitude for a Polite Planet,* chooses to explain civility by describing the behavior arising from its absence. She begins with common and seemingly minor annoyances, like interrupting when someone is talking; progressing to more serious infractions, such as a failure to express gratitude; and finally to the tragic realities of polarization and self-absorption. She then laments the scourge of cyber-bullying, pointing out its power to "leave teenagers so distraught that they believe their only recourse is to take their own lives."[2]

Having worked with teenagers for over twenty years, Hacala's observation about bullying hit a sensitive spot for me. I've sat for hours with these young souls, listening to them convey the harsh, hostile, and hateful things said and done to them by peers and parents. It seems a recent string of suicides connected to bullying is finally giving this issue the attention it deserves.

Civility is often understood less through direct definition or expression and more through words like *courtesy, manners, etiquette,* and *politeness.* These are helpful to arrive at a better understanding of civility's significance to the world. As civility professor P. M. Forni observes, "Whatever civility might be, it has something to do with courtesy, politeness, and good manners."[3] However, while these common concepts are similar, they're not the same.

First, courtesy is linked to the image of a royal court with its elegance and formality. Imagine the experience of preparing to meet the Queen of England, or, more popular these days, the royal baby. There are numerous behavioral dos and don'ts, all of which are intended to ensure your actions are consistent with the role of a courtier, or one who is in attendance at the royal court.[4] Even the official website for the British monarchy calls for guests meeting Her Majesty to "practice courtesy."[5] From its classical definition, courtesy is an exercise in bestowing respect by paying close attention to one's interaction with a person of superior status. In a modern context we would replace the monarch with someone to whom we are accountable: our boss, our parents, a judge, or someone else holding a position of honor and authority. On a personal and informal level, courtesy is an expression of humble deference to another. In this way we promote civil expression by putting the needs of others ahead of our own.

Second, the act of polishing brass, silver, or fine leather are images lending significance and meaning to the word, *polite.* The abrasive act clears away what obscures the object's brilliant beauty. Polishing must be repeated, for left unattended, the polished object's beauty will become obscured once again. In the same way, politeness takes constant work. Forni observes that polite people "have put some effort into bettering themselves."[6] While the French *civilite'* is often translated as politeness, Yale law professor Stephen Carter asserts that the word means more than merely being polite. It calls for a way of living that relates to others in a manner that promotes the advancement of civilization. "In short," writes Carter, "living in a way that is civilized."[7]

However, something can be polished in order to disguise its flaws or imperfections. Some polishes can work to cover up areas of weakness and deficiency, such as applying stain and polyurethane to rotten wood. Politeness has such a downside. Under the sheen of politeness, conflicts are addressed in a passive-aggressive manner. A co-worker offers a "polite" reply, under which anger boils. For various reasons, one tells a "polite" lie when asked for advice on an important decision. A less than stellar business presentation garners, at best, "polite" applause, or what comedians call "sympathy applause." Each of these glossed over responses "connect politeness to hypocrisy."[8]

Carter goes on to recount sinister actions that have been carried out through a twisted application of politeness. Segregation required black passengers to ride in the Jim Crow car and to use separate drinking fountains and restrooms. Women were forbidden to walk along the street alone or to vote: All as "simple matters of politesse."[9] In its purest meaning however, politeness remains such only as long as it does not become a tool of manipulation.

Third, many of us recall being told to get our elbows off the table, to wait until our guests are seated before we sit down, and to use our "inside voice," when talking. (In my household, we're still trying to help our son with the concept of utensils and saving his words until *after* he swallows his food.) We were reminded, begged, warned, and in my case often bribed to practice good *manners* as kids. Basic to good manners are offers of "please" and "thank you."

Like the previous words, manners are practiced out of regard and sensitivity to others, but the origin of the word encompasses far more than simply chewing with your mouth closed. *Manner* is derived from the Latin *manus*, meaning "hand." Manners are related to the use of one's hands, or in a more connotative sense, the manner by which something is *handled*. Forni again provides an observation, using the image of the hand:

> Thus manners came to refer to behavior in social interaction – the way we *handle* the encounter between Self and the Other. We have good manners when we use our hands well – when we handle others with care. When we rediscover the connection between *manner* and *hand*, the hand that, depending on our will and sensitivity, can strike or lift, hurt or soothe, destroy or heal, we understand the importance – for children and adults alike – of having good manners.[10]

Finally, while civility is incomplete without its connection to courtesy, politeness, and manners, it is superior to each of them. Civility is the proverbial glue that binds together a communal framework within which each of us interprets and interacts with others. Unless motivated by civility, there is little initiative to behave courteously, engage politely, and practice good manners. In a previous paragraph, Carter argued that *civilite'* is more than politeness. He goes on to explain the word "suggests an approach to life, a way of carrying one's self and relating to others – in short, living in a way that is civilized."[11]

Civility finds its origin in both the French *civilite'*, and the Latin *civilitas* and *civilis,* each expressing a life lived in relation to citizens. In the earliest records of its use, the term was connected to an idea of citizenship that included "good behavior, for the good of the community."[12] Richard Mouw, former president of Fuller Theological Seminary, confirms and expands the idea of civility as a vital component of social interaction. His thoughts contain the elements of politeness, manners, and courtesy; yet he also includes important essentials of fellowship and hospitality. These two are necessary for the relational aspect of civilized living. It's possible to practice politeness, good manners, and courtesy, yet remain detached, disconnected, and uninvolved in the life of the civilization. Mouw writes,

> In the past civility was understood in much richer terms. To be civil was to genuinely care about the larger society. It required a heartfelt commitment to your fellow citizens. It was a willingness to promote the well-being of people who were very different, including people who seriously disagreed with you on important matters. Civility wasn't merely an external show, it included an inner side as well.[13]

A commitment to the well-being of others also forms the heart of Aristotle's contribution to civility's development. Aristotle's idea of human beings as "political animals" is derived from the Greek word *polis,* pertaining to the city. Aristotle believed we realize our humanity only to the extent we function as good citizens of the *polis.*

Themes of hospitality and fellowship also emerge in Aristotle's view. He believed good citizens would live in relationships that moved beyond the parameters of familiarity and intimacy. In other words, we learn to live by extending courtesy to someone not because we are familiar them, but because we see them as fellow human beings, seeing them the way we see ourselves, and treating them accordingly. Aristotle believed that when we express our citizenship in this manner, "we have truly begin to flourish in our humanness."[14]

There is an important sacrificial foundation to civility. It is "the sum total of the many sacrifices we are called to make for the sake of living together."[15] By treating others civilly, we subject ourselves to each other and to the principles of humanity that underlie a common life together.

Sacrifice for the sake of others. Sounds a lot like what Jesus did for the world. It's something I learned from a girl we'll call "Grace."

Grace was new to our middle school. She didn't fit the "cool" profile in our tightly knit cliques. She was very quiet, and only spoke to me one time. Out of my own insecurity, I verbally bullied Grace without mercy. My friends thought it was hilarious. None of us knew her. She never said a word.

This went on for a few months. Then one Sunday night at church, my youth director said he wanted me to meet a new young lady. See, at church I was a leader in our youth group and I was supposed to help welcome new people. The new young lady was Grace. She looked at me and quickly looked at the floor. My youth pastor said to her cheerfully, "Kevin is one of our ambassadors, and I thought you'd like to get to know him since you are in the same grade." Grace looked in my eyes, and I heard her speak for the first time, "I know Kevin, he's the first person at school that spoke to me. Nice to see you, Kevin." Then Grace held out her hand. After an awkward pause I took it and looked at the floor. I've never forgotten that moment. She had every right to lash out at me. She would have been justified to tell my youth pastor how I'd treated her, to yell at me in front of the youth group, or respond in some other way to pay me back. But Grace was the bigger person. She was polite, she was courteous, and she was meek. Grace absorbed my incivility and opened her hand in an expression of all that makes civility both beautiful and essential. In doing so she exposed how ugly and destructive my incivility had been.

She and her family moved shortly after her visit to church and I never saw her again. I've thought a lot about Grace while writing this book and I've often wondered how many others like her have been the targets of uncivil, insecure, big-mouth bullies like me. I'm convinced there are too many.

Perhaps this is why displays of incivility, manifested in rude rhetoric, either/or propositions, vilification, or even inhumane violence has attracted the attention of so many. The shared sense of shock and dismay I and others experienced that fateful day in the parking lot of a Tampa gas station awakened the motivation for this invitation. In many areas of life, that same sense of dismay is an underlying reality in the face of an overwhelming problem of incivility present in our communities, our families, our corporations, on our highways, among our elected officials, and sadly, even in our churches.

Questions to Ponder

- Have you witnessed an event similar in severity to the one Kevin described at the gas station? What happened? How did you respond? What reflections would you offer in hindsight?

- Discuss the section, "What is Civility." In what ways were the descriptions of manners, politeness, and courtesy helpful? What, if any new information did you discover? In your own words, describe the similarities and differences between civility and manners, courtesy, and politeness. Why are these differences important?

- Talk about your initial reactions to the story about "Grace." Have you been a participant in uncivil behavior toward someone else? What would you do different? How will this reflection impact your future interactions?

- How does it strike you that the author openly struggles to practice the very principles shared in the book?

- Why did you choose this book? What do you and/or your discussion group hope to gain from this book? Talk about your goals.

- What was the most important takeaway from this chapter for you?

CHAPTER 2

It's an Uncivil World Out There.

*"We cannot do democracy without a heavy
dose of civility." - Mike Pence*

*"There are many men of principle in both parties in America, but
there is no party of principle.'
- Alexis de Tocqueville*

Political Incivility

Recently, speculations started to swirl about who will seek the Democratic Party's nomination for president in the 2016 election. 2016? Really? You can almost hear the collective sigh from citizens still stinging from the brutal election of 2012. When NBC and CNN announced plans for programming that chronicled the political career of Hillary Clinton, the Republican National Committee resolved to ban both networks from hosting Republican primary debates for the 2016 election.[16] Comedian Jay Leno quipped,

> The Republican National Committee now says if NBC and CNN don't pull plans for a Hillary Clinton miniseries and movie, they won't hold any Republican debates on those networks. That works for me! Now if we could just get the Democrats to

pull their debates, we wouldn't have to watch any
of that [stuff].[17]

The presidential election of 2012 reflected a polarization and
division in the "United" States, giving rise to what columnist
Kathleen Parker calls "a political era of uninhibited belligerence."[18]
Such a description is confirmed through a telling exchange between
Tempe, Arizona, Mayor Hugh Hailman and a group of pastors and
church leaders:

> The pressure, the heat, the level of hate over relatively
> insignificant issues has made civic leadership an
> almost impossible task. There is virtually no helpful
> discussion of issues. Instead, people feel obligated to
> undermine one another's character. [It's] corrosive
> vilification.[19]

President Obama recognized and addressed such a climate with
an appeal for civility as he urged men and women on opposing
political poles to "start thinking of each other as Americans first."[20]
Indeed, a call to recognize what those with differences have in
common would require us to listen, understand, and respond to others
in a way consistent with our own desire to be heard, understood, and
responded to: isn't there a rule about that somewhere?

To be sure, this is not an easy proposition, yet the United
States faces important if not daunting challenges of healthcare,
immigration, gun control, the economy, and other important issues.
These are problems that call for the best efforts of elected officials
and regular citizens whose common national identity could provide
a base of unity from which to discuss, debate, and decide a way
forward.

Few believe, however, that a place of unity can be found in such
a climate of incivility. *Time* magazine columnist Katy Steinmetz
wrote, "anyone hoping that the next Congress will usher in a

new era of civility, compromise and functionality will probably be disappointed."[21] Robert Parham, executive director of the Baptist Center for Ethics, began a post-2012 election article with a pessimistic outlook: "Last week's election results are now clearer. The political extremes will likely be meaner. The political center will likely be thinner. The prospects for civility and the common good will likely be bleaker."[22] Since civility is lacking, so too is political productivity. *Politico* columnist Roger Simon offers another concerned observation:

Compromise, which should be the very essence of our modern political system, is scorned. There is no desire for unity in our politics, only the desire to be re-elected. This means our politicians appeal to the extremes and not the middle –assuming such a middle actually still exists.[23]

Working in the middle for the common good is difficult when the extremes of opposing sides trade virtue for vilification, as blogger Gary Kinnaman observes, "It's not just that we disagree. No, we have to demonize each other."[24] Politicians are not the only ones exchanging civility for "corrosive vilification." The same problem exists in cubicles, boardrooms, and on the sales floors of the business world, and the toll it takes on workers and on the bottom line is sobering.

Workplace Incivility

The incivility displayed during the general election of 2012 was enough to raise awareness and begin conversations on the presence and problem of incivility. But it seems rudeness, meanness, bullying, and abusive behaviors in word and deed have been a problem in the workplace for quite some time. Incivility is being taken seriously as a workplace problem because of its negative effect on employee morale and productivity, which in turn diminishes the bottom line. In an article on civility in the workplace, puts it this way,

> While it can involve the bullying behavior of my experience, workplace incivility can also include such acts as interrupting a conversation, talking loudly in common areas, failing to return a phone call, checking email or texting during meetings, showing little interest in another individual's opinion, or even leaving malfunctioning office equipment for the next user to fix.[25]

After more than 10 years of research, and with data from 9,000 respondents, management researchers Christine Pearson and Christine Porath report on the serious effects of incivility on employee morale, corporate profits, and productivity:

- Nearly half of respondents were the target of incivility from a coworker at least once a week. That 2005 number had increased from about one-fourth of workers in their 1998 study.
- 95 percent reported experiences of incivility from coworkers.
- 12 percent said they have left jobs because they were treated badly.
- Fortune 1000 executives spend roughly seven weeks a year resolving employee conflicts.
- 80 percent of employees said they get no respect at work.

Not much imagination is required to think of the outcome of such widespread workplace incivility. According to Pearson and Porath, badly treated employees suffer more stress, lose energy, disengage, take more sick days or actually become ill with the stress. They also tell their coworkers about the bad behavior—causing anxiety and fear in colleagues who also may have to pick up the slack that results from lower morale and absenteeism. These perceptions are quite expensive and expansive as job stress costs

> U.S. corporations $300 billion a year, much of which has been shown to stem from workplace incivility. But incivility's true impact stretches far beyond that which is measurable in dollar terms ... incivility unleashes a set of complicated and destructive dynamics on individuals, teams, and organizations that impede performance and create organizational dysfunction on a number of levels, leading to diminished financial results.[26]

Ideally, workers can leave work at work, even if it's a negative atmosphere, and find peace and support at home with family. Unfortunately, for many households, home is as much a place of incivility as the office.

Incivility At Home

Family ties bind people together, yet those bonds are tested by the inevitability of familial conflict. Most would expect the majority of those problems to be resolved and the family would move forward. However, marriage and family therapist John Gottman reveals that families face what he calls perpetual problems: problems for which there is no resolution, or for which a resolution would come at the destruction of the relationship itself. Speaking specifically of married couples, Gottman writes, "An overwhelming majority (69 percent) of couples experience perpetual problems - issues with no resolution."[27]

While Gottman found perpetual problems to be pervasive among married couples, he also found the common approach in addressing such problems instrumental in leading many couples toward relational destruction. That approach, which involves all the elements of incivility, Gottman calls "gridlock."[28] Gridlock occurs when couples reach a point where they are unable to communicate with each other about the source of conflict. Because of the ongoing presence of the issue and the ongoing inability of the couple to communicate about it, the gridlock occurs over five digressive phases:

1. **Opposing Desires** – Desired outcomes that begin to take precedence over the value of the relationship itself, and fail to observe the way in which the conflict is tied to one's personality or sense of identity.

2. **Entrenchment** – A defensive posture whereby one or both parties "dig in," expecting an ongoing conflict. Here the value of winning the conflict has overtaken the value of the relationship. The other party is now an opponent from whom I must defend myself.

3. **Fear of Accepting Influence** – Conflict begins to affect areas outside of the issue itself. Overall suspicion toward the other begins to grow.

4. **Vilification** – Conflict becomes personal and pervasive. Motives of partner are seen in a more and more negative light. Relational history begins to be revised negatively.

5. **Disconnection** – A deliberate and defined break in the relationship.[29]

According to Gottman, the opposition that leads to gridlock is connected to very deep and personal desires that reside within the heart of every individual. These desires, or "dreams" as Gottman calls them, are rooted in the values that determine our very identity.[30] As a result, when these dreams or desires are threatened, we believe our human identity to be at stake. Fearing the damage that conflict might bring to their identity, the response is to drown out the person's voice altogether. As the list above illustrates, the defensive posture, suspicion, vilification, refusal to listen, and resulting relational disconnection are similar to what transpires in the uncivil interactions of business and politics. But in the home, it is perhaps an even more tragic turn of relational events, as the most severe forms of incivility can come from the people in whom we invest the most love and trust.

In addition, Gottman reveals another form of incivility in the home from which he is able to predict whether or not a couple will eventually divorce with 91percent accuracy after observing their interaction for just five minutes.[31] This destructive process results in conflicts for which there may indeed be a solution, but the manner of conversational posture, the lack of courtesy, politeness, and overall respect, bring about an environment of relationally deadly negativity. According to Gottman, "Certain kinds of negativity, if allowed to run rampant are so lethal to a relationship that I call them the Four Horsemen of the Apocalypse."[32] The Four Horsemen are:

1. **Criticism** – Moving beyond complaint to a critique of another's character or personality. It's working the person, not the problem.

2. **Contempt** (evidenced by sarcasm, cynicism, mockery, and belligerence) – A sense of superiority over the other. A demeaning and belittling posture toward the attempts of the other to participate in the conversation. Gottman considers this "the worst of the horsemen … because it conveys disgust."[33]

3. **Defensiveness** – One reacts by shifting blame to the other. Reasoning shuts down as one's body resorts to a fight or flight response.[34]

4. **Stonewalling** – A complete cutoff of conversation. No eye contact, physically turning away, and other physical signs that one has built a wall between them and the other.

Stonewalling becomes a default response over time, until the family is no longer able or willing to communicate. In family systems theory, this is known as "distancing," and is accompanied by unhealthy levels of engagement in activities that promote separation from the other. These include workaholism, over-engagement in hobbies, overuse of alcohol or other substances, and an increasing inability to relate well to other family members.[35] It is also a time when family members will often begin to turn to others outside the family for support or affirmation. Family Systems Theory call these Triangles, which can further complicate the relational dynamics, and can increase the chorus of incivility within the home.[36]

It could be argued that in business and politics, playing dirty can at times give us an immediate victory, but at what eventual cost? The "win" is at best temporary and often is revealed to be one that comes at the expense of corporate health, civic progress, or other expressions of the greater good. The same is true at home. When incivility erupts between siblings, spouses, and other family members, playing dirty may "win" the argument. But from a relational standpoint, what has been lost?

The thoughtful reader will see the many connections between Gottman's therapy for couples and other relationships in our lives. You definitely don't have to be married to have conflict with someone, experience gridlock, or to be trampled by the four horsemen.

Questions to Ponder

- Why do you think political discussions have become so volatile? Why would there be a sincere call for civility, but such difficulty convincing people to commit to civil discourse?
- Discuss the business expenses related to workplace incivility. What have you observed about the effect of civility (or lack thereof) on those in your workplace? If you are in leadership, how does it impact your ability to manage, lead, supervise, or otherwise execute your responsibility?
- Have you experienced the "gridlock" described in the chapter? What brought it on? How did you move past it?
- How would you describe the level of civility in your home? How does this help/hurt your interactions with loved ones?
- If you could change the environment in your home, what would it look like?
- To what extent have the "Four Horsemen" been a part of your communication practices? How have you witness the horsemen trample others?
- Has this chapter convinced you of the problems incivility poses to our society? If so, what do you think is at stake? If not, why not?
- What was the most important takeaway from this chapter for you?

CHAPTER 3

Incivility at Church – It's a Rough in Here Too.

We have a choice about how we behave, and that means we have the choice to opt for civility and grace." – Dwight Currie

"I know no religion that destroys courtesy, civility, and kindness."
- William Penn

Civility, according to Richard Mouw, is the choice to extend "public politeness" to others, even, perhaps especially, when we disagree with them. But civility and its supporting virtues are the result of a person's decision to embrace and extend them to others. While the goal of this book is to encourage and persuade you to express civility, it is an invitation you cannot be forced to accept. You and I must *want* to be civil. It can be expected and commended, but not demanded. Robert Pippin, American Philosopher and Professor at the University of Chicago, describes civility this way:

> Being civil to one another is much more active and positive a good than mere politeness or courtesy, but like many other important goods, such as generosity, gratitude, or solidarity, it is not the sort of thing that can be "demanded" as a matter of duty, like a moral entitlement.[37]

21

Could there be an exception to Pippin's statement? Is there a place in society from which civility could indeed be expected and demanded? I am convinced the answer to that question is, "yes."

It would seem reasonable that the Christian community would choose to obediently embody the civility present in Jesus' command to love God and your neighbor as you love yourself. The faith community then would be a living "sanctuary" from the hostility of the world. Within this sanctuary, believers encourage one another by learning what civility is and how it is lived out. We then enter the world where our civility contrasts with the coarseness of culture. The hope is that by our example of civility to each other and our civil posture toward the culture, our message of grace would become incarnational and invitational.

In reality, however, the community of faith does not resemble a living sanctuary. Instead, the Body of Christ has come to be seen as a pretty rough environment itself - more judgmental than incarnational, and more interested in conflict than compassion.

But is it really *that* bad? Has the culture's callous incivility really become a serious problem for the church and its people?

In 2009, public relations guru Mark Demoss launched The Civility Project, calling for greater civility in the public square. Demoss called on members of Congress as well as other influential people to commit themselves to greater respect in public discourse. In addition, Demoss, who is a devoted Christian, called on fellow Christians, churches, and church leaders to set the example for the rest of the country. After two years the project was shut down due to lack of participation. Demoss stated in an interview,

> The state of civil discourse in our country is, in my view, not good. In fact, it is generally terrible. This is not only a problem on the left among secularists; it is a problem on the right (sometimes worse so) and among people calling themselves followers of Christ.[38]

Bill Wilson, President of the Center for Congregational Health at Wake Forest University, calls the current state of congregational conflict a "pandemic." Wilson writes, "Our conflict intervention calls are on the upswing… conflict is surging."[39] Wilson goes on to explain that a primary culprit for this surge is the loss of civility in our culture: "Social scientists have documented the erosion of civility and social capital in a variety of settings. We find members of most congregations patterning their behavior in the church after the brutal tactics of our culture rather than on the teachings of Christ."[40] The Harford Institute for Religion Research reports that "75 percent of all churches report internal relational conflict within the past five years."[41] Kinnaman calls what he finds in more and more churches the "sin of incivility." He writes, "In the church, people are more often bound by an angry spirit of entitlement than by a Christ-like attitude."[42] Blogger Shawn Wood calls the current environment "The Christian Cannibal Culture," asking readers, "Do you ever just grow weary of something? Just throw your hands up and say, 'I'm tired of it'. Well, I am tired of the lack of civility, honor, and lingual responsibility shown to our Christian subculture."[43]

We see incivility expressed between Christian leaders. Theologian Roger Olson expressed concern over one pastor's accusations toward his colleagues: "This kind of venomous attack on fellow Christians, God-fearing, Bible believing, Jesus-loving Christians, is so uncalled for, so out of line, so indecent and uncivil that it demands censure."[44] While Olson raises the alarm, such an approach to disagreement within the Christian community is becoming increasingly common.

Incivility is also directed at pastors by parishioners. Charles Chandler is executive director of Ministering to Ministers, an organization that offers retreats to battered leaders. He reports shocking accounts of hostility and even violence directed toward pastors from church members. Chandler takes the problem seriously enough to call it an "epidemic" among churches.[45] I concur with Chandler's assessment. The worst treatment I've received as a minister has come not from atheists, agnostics, secular humanists, or even from a group of wiccans I know. I've been treated the worst by people within the church.

With words like cannibal, epidemic, pandemic, venomous, and sin used to describe the state of dialogue, discourse, and manner of disagreement among the Body of Christ, it isn't hard to conclude there is a significant problem of incivility in the church. It is a pressing problem, a tiring problem, a pervasive problem, and a problem that's been clearly and passionately identified. But what to do now? Responding with increased decibels of retaliation and demonizing rhetoric has simply deepened the polarization within the Body, and drastically reduced the church's voice in the culture.

We have a problem in the church. Here's my problem with the problem. I want to believe that someone else is more a part of the problem than I am. But if I'm honest, I know that I struggle with incivility. When a fellow Christian rubs me the wrong way, it's easier to react than it is to respond. *Washington Post* reporter Kelly Robinson shares a similar frustration, "The lack of civility in public discourse and by people of faith tempts me to incivility!"[46] Robinson's comment reveals how easy it can be for believers to simply fight uncivil fire with uncivil fire. Just like Kelly Robinson, my reaction is usually to play the game by the world's rules instead of practicing the way of Jesus. "As a Christian, I worry that many believers seem to be contributing more to the problem than the solution."[47]

Of course I'd love to see the problem of incivility solved, but as long as I believe YOU to be the problem there will be no solution. So I'm asking for your help. If I see myself as part of the problem and you see yourself as part of the problem, we can work together toward a solution that celebrates both our unity in Christ and the diversity of our place in the Body.

I have a friend who is a very talented mosaic artist. Much of her work is in finding the right kind of diversity of color, texture, shape, and size in the individual pieces. She tells me that a mosaic's unique beauty is in proportion to the difficulty of its assembly. She says her best works are stained with blood from her fingers. Her mosaics come to mind as I think about this problem.

The difficulty with the Body of Christ is its *diverse population* of broken humanity brought together through the grace of Jesus. In contrast, the beauty of the Body of Christ is its diverse population of broken humanity *brought together* through the grace of Jesus. On one hand, the broken pieces are sharp, rough and differ from one another, drawing blood from the hands working to create an image of unified diversity. The Body is a problematic project, "susceptible to division and fragmentation."[48] On the other hand, the broken lives redeemed by Jesus create a mosaic that reflects the creative unity of our Master Artisan. That's where I am hopeful.

Questions to Ponder

- Are you surprised at the level of incivility present in the church? Why or why not?
- To what extent have internal church "wars" damaged your faith or that of a friend or loved one?
- How have followers of Jesus hurt you? How have you processed, addressed, and dealt with the hurt?
- How has your own incivility within the church brought pain to someone else? What have you done to process, address, and deal with your actions?
- Why do you think the church can be such an uncivil environment? What are the factors that bring such hurtful words and actions from otherwise good-natured, rational people?
- What are your thoughts on the author's assertion that as long as we see incivility as another person's problem, the problem can never effectively be addressed?
- How does the metaphor of a Mosaic help you think through the contrasting realities of diversity and unity?
- What was the most important takeaway from this chapter for you?

PART 2

I remember as a kid seeing commercials for McGruff, the crime dog. His motto was, "Remember, we've all gotta work together to take a bite outta crime." I think McGruff was on to something. Crime is a problem too big for any one of us to solve on our own, but with each of us doing our part, crime can be (and statistically has been) decreased.

The problem of incivility requires the same approach. If each of us is willing to recognize the problem, take ownership of the problem, and work toward progress in our own lives, then I believe the church would see a significant difference overall. We could take a slice outta incivility … I know that was cheesy, but I bet you'll remember it!

What ideas are available and what help can those ideas offer Christians who recognize the problem of incivility and desire to improve their interaction? I think wisdom can be found from business, political, technological, and faith communities that offer ideas for solving incivility in their context. Some argue that the best solution is no solution at all, but a decision to manage the tension instead. Some, however, raise concerns that a posture of civility toward controversial issues is a slippery slope toward compromise and weakening of conviction.

The problem of incivility for the Christian community is one that occurs throughout the everyday life of the believer. Members of the Christian community are employees and employers, spouses and exes, students and teachers, friends and opponents, pastors and laity. Because the problem encompasses so many areas, the Body of Christ needs solutions to incivility that take seriously the health of a company, a church, a school, a home or other institution as well as the dignity and well-being of the people that populate them. For the Christ-follower, all of this includes the reality that those individuals are created in the image of God, and in many cases they are our brothers and sisters in Christ.

The purpose of this section is to examine proposed solutions to the problem of civility from a variety of perspectives. Each proposal has a foundational concern motivating the proponent's solution.

CHAPTER 4

Behavioral Bankruptcy and the Bottom Line

Memorial Day marks the beginning of grilling season for most Americans. When it comes to grilling for the Glenn family, however, it's a year-round affair. We live by the unofficial mantra of the U.S. Postal Service, not allowing snow, rain, or gloom of night to keep us from the grill's delights. When a winter storm dropped six inches of snow on our deck, I shoveled a path to the grill before I shoveled the driveway. Priorities.

So when it came time to purchase a new grill, you can imagine how serious I took the mission. After shopping around, I found the right grill for the right price at a home improvement store. I was ready to buy, but had a couple minor questions. I spent about ten minutes in the grill section with no employees offering to help. What I did see was a group of workers standing in a tight circle near the light bulbs. I approached and asked if I could get someone to answer a question about a grill I was ready to buy. Without making eye contact, one of them said, "Oh, you'll need to go over to the service desk." There was no one at the service desk. He and I both could see that. I mentioned this to the young man. He shrugged his shoulders, put his hands up and said, "I don't know."

That home improvement store has never again received my business. Since I've heard others share similar experiences about this chain, even hearing a late night talk show host make jokes about it, I have to wonder how such behavior impacts their bottom line. I've since learned that corporate or workplace incivility cuts deeply into the morale, productivity and bottom line of businesses.

"There is nothing productive about incivility, and the costs to us-individually, economically, and as a society-are astronomical."[49] So says etiquette coach, Sara Hacala. Her appeal includes a passionate plea for civil behavior, which she places against a backdrop of solid research across a wide spectrum of social interaction. Hacala weaves her solutions through 52 pithy and informative suggestions for creating a more "polite planet."

Creating a more polite planet involves taking seriously the difficult work involved in choosing to express civil behavior. "It is not simply enough to want the world to be a better place; we have to work at it, with a deep sense of purpose, commitment, courage, and compromise."[50] These well-articulated suggestions make good common sense. That is, if her suggested behaviors were commonly practiced, culture would indeed experience "greater respect, awareness, understanding, and acceptance of each other."[51] Such an observation makes clear what we *ought* to do regarding civility and taps into a sense of duty within humanity to make right what is perceived to be unfair, unjust, or inappropriate.

But not everyone shares that sense of duty. Keep in mind this appeal is being made to a culture that is not only rude, but increasingly so.[52] What about those who view civility as a sign of weakness?

> Many people see no need for civility in a less-than-perfect world. They believe that in our aggressive and competitive society civility is a luxury they cannot afford. If you are polite, you are perceived as weak and you are brushed aside, they say. Being considerate and kind is hazardous to your self-esteem, your ambitions, and your net worth.[53]

A call to a culture with a declining sense of duty and an increasing belief that civility is a sign of weakness may convince us that to express civility is an exercise in futility. Therefore, workplace civility may be difficult to incentivize on merits of duty, but the shrinking profits of companies with uncivil working environments are sufficient to motivate change in the practices, processes, and eventually the personality of the organization and its people. In other words, when workers have no incentive to learn how to behave in a more civil manner, money talks.

Because of the massive corporate cost connected to incivility, businesses don't just call for civility on grounds of its impact on the social environment (employee morale). They also point to success for all involved when employees feel valued, respected, understood, and accepted. In a study on five corporations modeling admirable levels of workplace civility, management coaches Christiane Pearson and Christine Porath reveal, "Each of them is cultivating civility within its workplace, and each attributes at least part of its success to that fact."[54] In addition to the financial aspect of cost to uncivil companies, their study addresses the emotional, physical, and social connections between the health of the person and the health of the corporation. As basketball legend John Wooden once said, "The main ingredient of stardom is the rest of the team." If one line could sum up Pearson and Porath's perspective it would be that "there are costs for bad behavior."[55] Since people are responsible for behavior, corporate issues are people issues. In this way, suggested solutions to incivility from the world of business could be of great value to Christians seeking to improve civility within their own places of work, and for Christian leaders seeking to address the problem of incivility within the church itself.

Through their website and blog,[56] and their popular book, *The Cost of Bad Behavior*, Pearson and Porath offer specific advice for people affected by incivility in various ways. There are steps for corporations to confront and change a hostile work environment,[57] instructions for department leaders which outline how to address incivility among direct reports, and tips on how to pick up signs of hostility when interviewing potential employees.[58]

An important part of addressing workplace incivility is what to do if you are a victim. Contrary to popular metaphors that compare workplace hostility to playground bullying, the best advice is not to "fight back." Instead, engage in a measured and strategic process that offers the best chance for a positive outcome. Such a process addresses the issue itself, keeping the situation professional rather than personal.[59]

For the Christian community, there are some important lessons to take from this solution. First, insistence that targets not retaliate in a "school playground" manner is consistent with Jesus' instructions regarding conflict in Matthew 18. The offended party is to follow a process that allows for a redemptive and optimistic outcome. The offended party is seeking above all to reach a conciliatory end to the conflict. Both in the Body of Christ and in the business world retaliation only works to escalate the conflict to a scenario where everyone loses. Hence, God is clear that acts of vengeance fall into his department alone.

A second lesson for the church is found in the manner of keeping conflict centered on the behavior instead of the person. This approach seeks to protect the relationship with a fellow brother or sister in Christ while at the same time honestly addressing an issue of disagreement. It is important for members of the Body to remember above all else that while we may indeed need to decisively address, resist, and even reprimand incivility, the one we are addressing remains a fellow member of the faith community. The relationship may indeed be strained to the point that interaction or employment is eliminated, but keeping the issue about the issue and not the person allows for the optimism of a redemptive and peaceful outcome, if not immediately, perhaps eventually.

With redemption and optimism in mind, there is hope for offenders who realize the toll their incivility is taking and who are willing to pay the price necessary to correct their behavior.

Recovering offenders must face the difficult reality of their actions by gathering data collected from their peers, opening themselves to coaching, and if needed, counseling. Finally, offenders should begin forming new habits of interaction based on responding instead of reacting.[60]

For both victims and offenders, long-term change is only possible when problem habits are replaced by healthy habits. Victims may need to address habitual patterns of passivity and low self-respect, exchanging them for practices of healthy assertiveness and confidence. Incivility may be an expression of humility and deference, but it is in no way intended to be mistaken for weakness.

In a related issue, some victims may not be the targets of deliberate incivility, but instead may be overly sensitive to particular social environments. A study out of the University of Houston found that some people believing themselves to be targets of incivility were inappropriately reacting to very normal conditions. They had in common habits of social detachment, of being easily irritated or offended, and of expressing a high degree of insecurity. The study suggests that managers not only train workers to develop habits of civility, but to also provide help in developing habits of properly interpreting appropriate workplace interaction.[61] Offenders, on the other hand, need to replace habits of aggressiveness and insensitivity with habits consistent with civility and respect.

When both victims and offenders practice new and better habits of interaction, the benefits to the organization reach farther than simple kindness at the water cooler. The entire culture of the organization can change. Charles Duhigg calls these "Keystone Habits."[62] Keystone habits trigger change in areas beyond the specific problem the new habit is targeting.[63] When one part improves, the whole organization becomes stronger.

It is no accident that the apostle Paul uses the metaphor of a body to describe the interaction between "members" of the Body of Christ. Much like Duhigg's keystone habits, it can be difficult to understand how parts of the Body that seem so different from one another would actually depend on each other. Paul's use of the body alludes to a well-known fable in his day credited to Aesop called *The Belly and its Members*.[64] It concerns an imaginary dispute between the stomach and other body parts. The "members" are fed up because the stomach gets all of the food. In retaliation, the members refuse to supply the stomach with food, until they realize they are becoming weak themselves. The members finally understand their connection to the stomach, and all ends well. In like manner, when deliberate steps are taken to respect and better understand each member, the whole body flourishes.

Civility within the Body of Christ is a problem for each member, since each member is an offender. As such, each member bears part of the responsibility toward the solution to the problem. The suggestions available in this chapter hold great value for addressing corporate incivility. Followers of Christ in the business world can benefit greatly from these principles as they display glimpses of the Kingdom in their work toward creating a more polite planet.

Christians involved in church or nonprofit ministries can apply these principles, since it takes both human and monetary resources to do ministry: "Workplace incivility is not only a problem reserved for large corporations. It occurs across the spectrum, including in religious institutions."[65] Declining financial involvement or a dwindling volunteer base can often be traced to leaders, staff, volunteers, benefactors and others who sense a lack of respect, sensitivity, understanding, and civility even within a religious organization's environment. Therefore, the problem of incivility, being present in for-profit businesses, non-profit organizations, and in church-based ministries can indeed be addressed through the solutions above.

Questions to Ponder

- Why do you think some view civility as a sign of weakness? How would you suggest that it is not?
- How do you respond to the financial incentives some companies provide in order to insure a civil workplace is maintained? Discuss those implications within your own context. Would this be something you'd consider? Why or why not?
- How have you witnessed the "school playground" type of retaliation between followers of Jesus? What was the outcome of such escalation?
- To what extent would you equate incivility with bullying? How are they similar? How are they different?
- Discuss how victims can make positive and productive strides to oppose incivility. If you have been a victim, what did you do?
- Discuss what you believe to be the "Keystone Habits" in your workplace or organization related to improved civility. What else would change for the better if these were addressed?
- In your workplace, what measures are in place to curb incivility? How could these be applied to a family? To a church?
- What was the most important takeaway from this chapter for you?

CHAPTER 5

The Solution in the Sign

"I know that you believe you understand what you think I said, but I'm not sure you realize that what you heard is not what I meant." - Robert McCloskey

"You keep using that word. I do not think it means what you think it means"– Indigo Montoya

One of my favorite games to pass the time is an app on my phone called the "logo quiz." The object is to name the company as quickly as possible with only its logo appearing. I've found the logos I get the fastest are those with whom I have a story or an experience to connect with it. For example, the logo for an exotic car came and went without my recognition, but a logo with mouse ears came to mind immediately. Why? The logo for an exotic sports car held no story for me. The mouse ears, however, immediately flooded me with images and emotions. Disney is practically an extension of my family. I could write books on the stories and experiences connected with the image of those mouse ears. The image is a symbol, representing experiences, emotions, identities, dreams, and other much deeper and wider things than the image itself could ever convey.

When we deliberately look for the deeper and wider significance of signs, be they pictures, gestures, objects, people, locations, logos, words, or even literal signs by the road, we are practicing what I believe to be one of the most important and overlooked tools we have for understanding each other. I'd like to introduce you to something called *semiotics* (Sim-ee-o-tics).

Semiotics is a fancy way of talking about perceptions. It helps us understand another person's "collateral experience," a phenomenon we'll explain below, and in so doing, helps us address the problem of incivility.

Semiotics is an attempt to understand the way we humans communicate through the use of signs. When we think of signs we think of something visual like a stop sign. But, "signs" are made up of many different components - words, sounds, body language and context. These components combine to create a *visual language* which helps us interpret the sign's message.

Semioticians, not only study "signs"- we study how meaning is formed. We study how people interpret a sign and how we then draw on cultural and personal experience to understand a sign. Semiotics then, is tied closely to communication.

Signs are understood to be both visual and verbal. When you come to a stop sign, both the red octagon metal part, and the text "stop" are equal parts of the sign that instructs a motorist to hit the brakes. Semiotic pioneer, Ferdinand de Saussure (1857-1913, a Swiss linguist, proposed that "a sign has two parts: a signified concept in the mind and the signifier that generates the concept."[66] For the driver then, the *signified* concept in the mind would be the concept of stopping their vehicle. A concept learned for the sake of safety to their person, property, and that of others.

The *signifier*, in Saussure's view, would be the stop sign itself. However, a sign's significance can change because of time, culture, or other factors. English and film studies professor Crystal Downing describes Saussure's perspective: "Like ingredients drawn from a cupboard, meaning is drawn from a sign's context."[67]

Saussure's dyadic, or two-fold (signifier/signified) system dominated the science during the twentieth century, also impacting rhetoric, anthropology, psychology, philosophy, theology, and art criticism. Over time, however, others studying semiotics challenged Saussure's dyadic system, believing it too narrow to understand the complexities surrounding a sign's meaning.

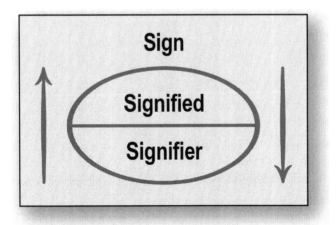

Figure 1: Saussure's Dyadic System

A contemporary of Saussure, American philosopher C.S. Peirce (1839-1914), developed a triadic (three-fold) view of the sign. This was an important development because the additional concept allowed for understanding "a world beyond language."[68] For Peirce, this made room for more than just the sign and what it signifies (stop the car). It allows for other responses rising from a person's personal context. This third aspect helps explain why signs trigger responses that go beyond the simple signifier/signified relationship.

Let's go back to our stop sign for an example. Suppose you are riding along in the car with the driver. Suddenly, the driver bursts into tears at seeing and reading the stop sign! You would wonder what's happening. It's just a stop sign, right? But it would be clear to you that there is deeper significance to this stop sign than you are aware of. So you ask, "What's wrong?" and learn the driver's mother was recently killed in an accident caused by someone running a stop sign. Now there is an entirely different understanding between the driver and the passenger when they approach a stop sign.

Whereas Saussure's dyadic sign considered only the signifier and the signified, Peirce considered the addition of objects that the sign refers to. "Any sign has *two Objects,* its object as it is represented and its object in itself."[69] Peirce calls the object as it is perceived the "representamen." This is the sign as it is perceived to the person. In our example it is the stop sign's significance to the driver.

The object in itself is the physical stop sign as it exists; red, white, metal, and octagonal, with the letters s-t-o-p. This is the stop sign as perceived by the passenger. To one the object is laden with additional representations. To the other the same object represents only the significance of stopping. The difference, according to Peirce, is in the "interpretant; the person's mental apprehension of the object."[70] The stop sign (object) then, is as much a sign (representamen) of carelessness, recklessness, loss, and pain for the driver (interpretant) as the same stop sign (object) is merely a sign (representamen) to stop (interpretant) for the passenger. This triadic process inspired by Peirce is part of what is taught today as the "semiotic triangle."[71] Peirce however, called the process the "triadic relation."[72]

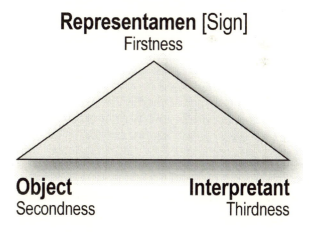

Representamen [Sign]
Firstness

Object
Secondness

Interpretant
Thirdness

Figure 2: Peirce's Triadic Relation

Taking the time to nail down these concepts will open up an expansive new understanding into how much is really going on when we attempt to communicate. You'll be able to make sense between what someone says and what another person hears. You'll also be able to understand why this happens and have the tools to help untangle the communication lines that so easily trip us up. More importantly, you will better understand how you hear what others say and how you can be understood more effectively.

This raises the question of understanding. If a sign can be "heard" or interpreted in a multitude of different conceptions by others, what then creates the differing interpretations? According to Peirce, it is "collateral experience" or "collateral observation," both of which refer to "the prerequisite for getting any idea signified by the sign...a previous acquaintance with what the sign denotes."[73]

Back at the stop sign, you, the passenger are incapable of understanding how the stop sign has come to elicit a response (bursting into tears) you interpret as unusual from the driver, without knowledge of the driver's experience of loss. On the other hand, the driver could interpret your bewilderment at their emotional outburst as insensitive. The collateral experience is for the driver "a previous acquaintance with what the sign denotes" (the accident resulting in the loss of the driver's mother.) However, this is unknown to you because the experience is "a prerequisite to getting any idea signified by the sign."

This is why semiotics is important. It helps us understand collateral experience in ourselves and others as we work toward a solution to the problem of incivility. It is often our failure to understand how words are perceived that escalates a situation to the point of incivility. As semiotics helps illuminate the inner workings of perceptions, it helps us understand how to say what we're trying to say in a way that others "get" what we're saying. The study of semiotics provides a valid and necessary element to a foundation for understanding communication, and by extension is a valuable skill for civil conversation.

The field of semiotics, while affecting communication, remains a little known or little understood discipline among many within both the secular and Christian communities. Efforts are underway within the realm of Christian education to increase the awareness and demonstrate the relevancy of semiotics for the future of church ministry. However, a strategic, simplified, and applicable process for exposing semiotics and its benefits as an accessible toolbox for civil and productive dialogue is needed for the Body of Christ. I hope this brief primer on semiotics helps us better understand our own collateral experience, as well as understanding the experience behind the words and responses of our Christian brothers and sisters. Equipped with such tools, perhaps we can build more bridges and fewer walls.

Questions to Ponder

- Talk through your understanding of Semiotics after reading this chapter. Had you heard of it before? How would you describe Semiotics to a friend?
- How has this chapter helped you understand communication?
- Talk about some words, phrases, or signs that have a powerful meaning to you. Share the backstory, or "collateral experience" that makes this so.
- Think through an intense argument, debate, or disagreement you've witnessed or been a part of recently. How would an understanding of semiotics have helped the conversation? What unnecessary escalation took place because collateral experience wasn't considered? How would such an understanding aid in reconciliation?
- A great resource for further discovery of Semiotics and its application to the Christian community, check out Crystal Downing's *Changing Signs of Truth: A Christian Introduction to the Semiotics of Communication.*
- What was the most important takeaway from this chapter for you?

CHAPTER 6

Making Music in the Middle

"Most of us would like our faith to reduce tension. But, according to Jesus (who told us to be anxious for nothing but always alert, to be last in order to be first, to be weak to be strong, and to lose our lives to find them), tension is required."- Carolyn Arends

"A vibrant faith may necessitate oscillation and tension. In the absence of motion, there's no music. - Music Producer Roy Salmond

My 16- year-old daughter routinely sticks her thumb in her eye to remove contact lenses. It's fascinating to me that her thumb is able to gently remove the small plastic lens from that most sensitive part of the body. On the other hand, a major league baseball pitcher is able to use the tension of their thumb to aid in throwing a 100-mph fastball. Both actions are possible because of the right amount of tension.

I spent many years living near the Sunshine Skyway Bridge over Tampa Bay. The structure is a striking feat of beauty and function, and it is another example of necessary tension. Leonard Sweet observes, "unless the forces of compression and tension are present in the correct proportions, the bridge would collapse."[74] The opposing forces of pushing and pulling are necessary for one to take the practical route of getting to work, and for another to marvel at its beauty. Some of the most beautiful music we hear comes from the tension produced when hammers strike the strings of a piano, a bow presses and drags across the taunt strings of a cello, or the skilled fingers of a guitarist press, pluck and strum. Whether it is the relief of taking out a contact, the thrill of a ballgame, the beauty and function of a bridge or the excitement of a concert, tension is actually needed for life to function and be enjoyable. Is it possible to simply allow the paradox of opposing tensions to be a source of civil and productive dialogue rather than a source of rudeness and relational strain? Advocates of polarity management suggest it is not only possible; it is necessary to the success of both an organization and a relationship. Developer of polarity management Barry Johnson, introduces his concept as follows:

> I have some bad news and some good news. The bad news is that you have some unsolvable problems in your life, both at work and at home. I'm not talking about difficulties you could solve if you had more money, time, or other resources. I'm talking about ones that are inherently unsolvable. The good news is that you can stop trying to solve them.[75]

There is energetic tension in every relationship because of the different experiences and unique emotional associations every person has with his or her experiences. The process of using words to identify what common ground may or may not exist between two people or among a community of people is the best we can do to manage that tension. Unfortunately, the very words we use to communicate are often laden with baggage and associations themselves, making it necessary for words to be chosen with care, caution, and sensitivity to the collateral experience attached to the word. Business, churches, service groups, sports teams, and even families contain members with different points of view and different cultural perspectives. These different perspectives trigger diversity issues that lead to tension, strained relationships, anxiety, hostility, and a lack of respect, understanding, and sensitivity - the recipe for incivility. At the core of such dysfunction is an inability to distinguish between a problem to be solved, and a polarity (tension, dilemma, paradox) to be managed. Knowing the difference, however, makes all the difference.

> Polarities are interdependent opposites which work best when both are present to balance each other. Polarities are on-going; have no end point; are not solvable; and need each other over time to optimize a situation."[76]

Polarities consist of a set of opposing ideas that are unable to function well independent of each other. They are interdependent opposites. "Because the two sides of a polarity are interdependent, you can't choose one as a 'solution' and neglect the other. The objective of the Polarity Management perspective is to get the best of both opposites while avoiding the limits of each."[77]

Polarity management's importance for the problem of civility goes beyond helping one politely consider a different point of view. It is a profitable tool for distinguishing between a problem with a definitive solution and a polarity that exists as part of a dynamic and relational tension that ebbs and flows. Like a suspension bridge or a tuned guitar, such a dynamic tension can be understood to give flexible strength, harmonious coordination, and successful progress to the organization from every point on the continuum. In the example below, Johnson demonstrates the interdependent polarities of inhaling and exhaling:[78]

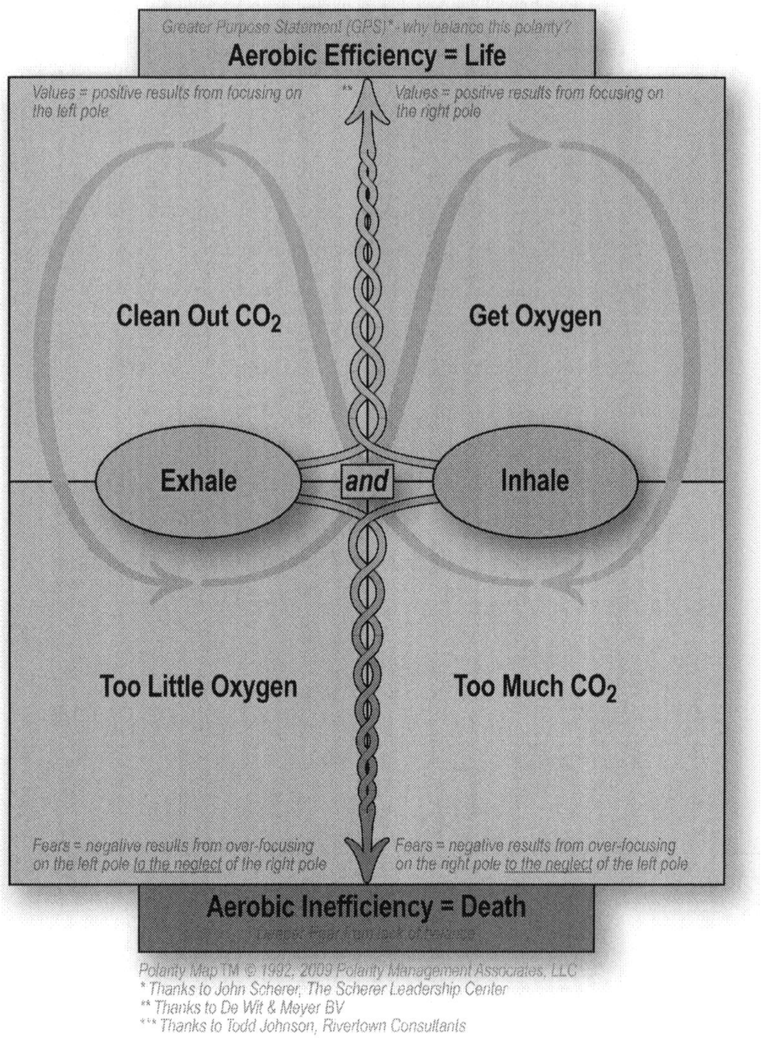
Greater Purpose Statement (GPS)* - why balance this polarity?
Aerobic Efficiency = Life
Values = positive results from focusing on the left pole
**
Values = positive results from focusing on the right pole
Clean Out CO_2
Get Oxygen
Exhale
and
Inhale
Too Little Oxygen
Too Much CO_2
Fears = negative results from over-focusing on the left pole to the neglect of the right pole
Fears = negative results from over-focusing on the right pole to the neglect of the left pole
Aerobic Inefficiency = Death
Polarity MapTM © 1992, 2009 Polarity Management Associates, LLC
* Thanks to John Scherer, The Scherer Leadership Center
** Thanks to De Wit & Meyer BV
*** Thanks to Todd Johnson, Rivertown Consultants

The image of a child on a swing is another example of this necessary and productive tension. The actions of kicking forward while leaning back are opposite movements, yet they are interdependent. Some of us might value kicking forward, while others value leaning back, but without both, the swing doesn't move.

Our view of any given situation is driven from what is valued, a motivational value, or a preferred pole. What is unknown, or what we are typically blind to, is our non-preferred pole, also known as the motivational value's independent pair.[79]

Figure 4: "Parabolic Harmonious Oscillation"

Physicists call this "parabolic harmonious oscillation," but the term is captured and applied by Leonard Sweet to the necessity for Christ followers to navigate the tension of polarities and paradox. He calls paradox "the midwife of truth,"[80] and urges Christians to be the most prepared people for the paradoxical realities of the future. He goes on to suggest that paradox is the source of true beauty:

We see the unseen
We subdue by submitting
We win by losing
We are made grand by making ourselves little
We come in first by becoming last
We are honored by being humble
We fill up with God by emptying out ourselves
We become wise by being fools
We possess all things by having nothing

We wax strong by being weak
We find life by losing ourselves in others
We live by dying. [81]

How does one identify a polarity? Johnson suggests two
questions. First, is the difficulty one that continues to resurface?
Second, are there two poles that are interdependent? Andy Stanley,
when teaching on a similar issue, added an additional question: Are
there mature advocates on both sides?[82]

There is merit to Stanley's additional question. The character
of the individuals on either side of the polarity allow for relational
integrity and serve as a catalyst for the necessary civil dialogue that
must take place for the polarity to be managed well.

Johnson's practices have helped many organizations navigate
their unsolvable problems with great success. His coaching company
now certifies individuals to take his principles into their own
contexts. In 2010, Johnson partnered with Lutheran pastor Roy
Oswalt to develop *Managing Polarities in Congregations*, a resource
for churches.

> Congregations often find themselves in power
> struggles over two opposing views. People on both
> sides believe strongly that they are right. They also
> assume that if they are right, their opposition must
> be wrong -- classic 'either/or' thinking. A polarity is a
> pair of truths that need each other over time. When
> an argument is about two poles of a polarity, both
> sides are right and need each other to experience
> the whole truth.[83]

Bill Wilson, in reference to Oswalt's book, suggested,

> Many of the most vexing issues we face as
> congregations will never be addressed in a healthy

fashion by either/or thinking. It is only when we embrace the proverbial "genius of the and" that we can have a transforming impact for Christ upon our people and our culture.[84]

In order for a pianist, a violinist, or a guitarist, to bring music from the tension of string, they have to play with hands that grip the pick, the bow, or hands arched to strike the keys. But they also must have hands that are open and flexible. Hands able to move and adjust to the changing movement of the song:

> When we are asked to hold two seemingly opposite truths in tension, we experience confusion (which can be painful) before we get to any sort of cohesion. So, we often bail and settle for one pole or the other, congratulating ourselves for taking a stand, but losing at least half of what God has for us in the process.[85]

Polarity management is also useful for navigating the often conflicted seasons of transition in both organizational and personal life. When runners compete in a relay race the transition of handing off the baton can make or break the forward momentum. We in the Christian community are positioned to either hand the baton to the next generation or to take the baton and run forward. In some ways we are likely doing both. There is a moment in the transfer when the advancing runner must reach back while the retiring runner must reach forward. These moments are critical and the opposite forces of pressure and release, taking off and slowing down, and giving and taking must be managed well. If we don't pay attention to these interdependent opposites the transition fails and momentum falters.

Transitions can become moments of failure because of fear. Rudolph Bahro observed, "When an old culture is dying, the new culture is created by those people who are not afraid to be insecure."

Transitions are times of vulnerability, uncertainty, and risk. Yet the race cannot continue without transitions. How do we manage the tension of a changing course, of different ways to run, or of a new pace? What is the best hope for the race ahead?

The apostle Paul offers great coaching here, "Do you not know that in a race all the runners run, but only one gets the prize? Run in such a way as to get the prize."[86] Run with abandon, run without fear, run with confident insecurity, run with the knowledge that the past is history and the future is an adventure. Run in a way that blazes a trail for others who will follow your path when your time is over. Run in the redemptive tension between the past you learn from and the future you create.

Questions to Ponder

- One of the hardest things for a problem solver like me to process is the reality of unsolvable problems! How about you? Talk about the presence of unsolvable problems. Do you struggle admitting them? What problems in or around your life would might be unsolvable?

- Discuss some issues for which you've only considered an "either/or" solution. Which of these contain "interdependent opposites?"

- What might need to change in your own perspective in order for the polarities to be managed, rather than the problem to be "solved?"

- Many churches struggle with conflict. How could Polarity Management help your own faith community address problems in a more civil and productive manner?

- Discuss parabolic harmonious oscillation ... okay, first say it three times really fast. How can we lean into the past while reaching out toward the future? How can this image help churches and other organizations manage the present tension between the past and future?

- In what ways might Polarity Management be of help to your family and other close relationships? For more on this, check out John Gottman's *7 Principles for Making Marriage Work*, specifically, the section on "Overcoming Gridlock."

- What was the most important takeaway from this chapter for you?

CHAPTER 7

A Moral Compass in Cyberspace

*"It has become appallingly obvious that our technology
has exceeded our humanity." – Albert Einstein*

*"Most of us present an enhanced image of ourselves on Facebook.
This positive image—and the encouragement we get, in the form of
"likes"—boosts our self-esteem. And when we have an inflated sense
of self, we tend to exhibit poor self-control." – Elizabeth Bernstein*

In 2012, Notre Dame Linebacker and Heisman trophy nominee
Manti Te'o was hailed for his courage to play in the face of the tragic
death of his grandmother and his girlfriend. While his grandmother's
death was a real event, it was later discovered that Te'o's girlfriend,
her graduation from Stanford, her illness, and her death were false.
All of it was the result of an elaborate online identity, complete with
photos, a Twitter account, an Instagram page, a Facebook page,
and phone calls. Te'o admits he never met the woman in person,
but developed a close relationship with her. A former friend of Te'o
eventually admitted to creating the whole thing, although it is still
unclear if Te'o was a participant, a victim, or something in between.

The incident ignited conversations regarding the ease of creating
a false identity online, the ethics of doing so, and the impact such
behaviors have on individuals and communities. The connection
between civility and morality effectively frame the issues raised in

the brave new world of social media. What was most surprising for me was how often this same situation is taking place today: often enough for MTV to feature a show called *Catfish TV*, which films men and women who explore, discover, and confront their online deceivers. Manti Te'o simply brought to light a phenomenon that happens with regularity in our online world, a world where electronic screens alter the standards of reality, morality, and civility.

Andrea Weckerle, attorney and founder of Civil-nation, a non-profit organization specializing in online hostility, offers a perspective on the growing incivility in cyberspace. More than 30 percent of the world's population now uses the internet. That's roughly two billion users, representing 340 undecillion (340 trillion trillion trillion) unique IP addresses.[87] It's little wonder, according to Weckerle, the number of online insults found on Twitter alone were compared to resemble "a weaver-bird colony at dawn."[88]

To be sure, cyber incivility is a problem for the church as well. The world of instant communication has made it all too easy to pass on rumors or engage in reactionary rhetoric. Christians often "get drawn into wars of online words, and before they know it, they've inadvertently done more harm than good."[89]

I agree that it's easy to text, post, tweet, or otherwise communicate online in an inadvertently uncivil way. Because I can let my fingers do the talking before my brain and heart catch up, I have a habit of letting my online posts "cool" before I send them. I wait a little while and read back over what I planned to send. I find that I don't send most of what I had planned to.

On the other hand, there are deliberately uncivil, untrue, and even malicious things posted online by Christians about other Christians. Just a quick look into the comment thread of many Facebook pages, blogs, and other online interactions will reveal a shocking level of hostility among members of the cyber-Body of Jesus. My mentor, Leonard Sweet is the subject of sites dedicated to discrediting and labeling him as a New Age heretic.[90] I was the target of a Facebook page back in 2008 intended to portray me as a false teacher to the parents and students of the ministry I was serving. These were not "inadvertent" examples of friendly fire.

To begin addressing this problem, it helps to understand who the troublemakers are. The largest category are the "trolls," whom Weckerle describes as "attention-seekers whose sole goal is to wreak havoc online for fun and pleasure ... they thrive on the perceived weakness and naiveté of their victims. They delight in insulting, shocking, upsetting, and provoking others."[91]

Another category of online troublemaker is the "sock puppet." Like trolls, sock puppets are committed to incivility, but do so under false identities, much like those involved in the Manti Te'o incident. "The reason for using a sock puppet is to be intentionally deceptive, whether for purposes of entertainment, to undermine or attack an opponent, or to gain social political, or business advantage."[92] In her call for cyber civility, Weckerle appeals to a moral mandate, stating that users should measure their online behavior in light of the values held by society, one of which she believes is civility.

Whether we are online or engaged in face-to-face interaction, the ethical maturity required for us to choose civility is both complex and difficult, requiring that we learn to understand the impact of our decisions. "With a training in civility we develop the valuable habit of considering that no action of ours is without consequences for others and anticipating what those consequences will be."[93] It can be difficult however, for consequences to be grasped in a culture where self-expression and self-esteem are valued over self-control.

> As a society we have done a good job of encouraging self-esteem but not a good job of teaching self-control. We all need self-esteem. Self-esteem is good, it keeps us sane, it is an immune system for our souls. However, when we are too focused on raising self-esteem, we swell the ranks of the self-absorbed.[94]

The way forward is found in a civility that reflects the Christ-like traits of moral conviction and compassionate sacrifice. Yale law professor Stephen Carter writes, "Civility is a moral issue, not just a matter of habit or convention: It is morally better to be civil than to be uncivil."[95] Carter understands civility to be an expression of societal sacrifice and believes all of us are morally responsible to put the other ahead of self. Civility calls for us to extend politeness, courtesy, and good manners out of a conviction that doing so is necessary for one to be a good neighbor within the larger community. Civility is a morally mandated awareness, "an active interest in the well-being of others." A tapestry into which is woven restraint, respect, and consideration of others. As such, "civility belongs in the realm of ethics."[96]

The decision to practice civility is also supported by the belief that we as individuals populating society will reap the positive benefits of it. Those who practice civility discover again and again that "being kind is good for the kind."[97] Civility is good for the individual and good for the whole of society online and offline. Civility allows our self-esteem to develop with a healthy dose of humility, and our self-expression to develop with restraint. Civility is sacrificial, a selfless quality necessary for human flourishing. Yet civility remains an invitation. We can choose not to pursue civility, and many make this choice.

But I am optimistic. I am hopeful. I believe that expressing civility to others will in some way impress them to adopt and express it themselves. "By treating you the best way I know how, I appeal to the best in you, urging you to do the same. The practice of civility is the applying of gentle force with the goal that everybody be a winner in the delicate game of social exchange."[98]

While such a posture appeals to the optimist in me, I am also realistic. The experience of 23 years in church ministry have proven time and again that treating others the best I can and applying the gentle force of kindness is not a sure-fire motivator toward civility, and at times has been returned with a torrent of anger, vitriol, and uncivil rhetoric. In an effort to prepare civil people for those who respond to the gentle pressure above with uncivil behavior, P.M. Forni wrote *The Civility Solution: What to do When People are Rude.* This work offers an entire section on what it means to accept everyday rudeness while maintaining our own sense of respect and safety. Yet Forni holds stubbornly to his optimism, and so will I. "Why spend time on something that does not benefit us directly? Because it is the right thing to do…Civility compels us-at least some of us-to stand."[99] Whether face-to face, or online, will you stand for a morally convicted, sacrificially compassionate, Christ-like civility?

Questions to Ponder

- Discuss the merits of letting an online comment, post, text, tweet, or email "cool" before sending. Have you ever sent something online you wish you could "un-send?" What are the pros and cons of a cool-down period?

- The internet is an easy way to spread rumors. One of the biggest culprits are hoaxes or false accusations that are carelessly forwarded without verification. Before you hit "forward," "retweet," or "share," what actions do you take to verify the accuracy of the information? When you receive something you know to be false, how do you correct it? Have you discovered snopes.com?

- How far should a disagreement go between two Christ-followers online? What do you think the boundaries for public debate should be? Discuss what you have seen (both positive and negative) in online dialogue.

- How would you gauge your level of civility online? Would you say to the person's face, what you're writing on their wall?

- Talk about the sacrificial nature of civility. How does this play out in real life? In what ways does civility call for us to put aside what might be a justified retaliation?

- In light of the moral and sacrificial elements of civility, do you think civility too high an expectation for Christ followers? Why or why not?

- What was the most important takeaway from this chapter for you?

CHAPTER 8

"Friendly" Fire – It Hurts Us All

"Why can't we all just get along?" – Rodney King

"Put first things first and we get second things thrown in:
Put second things first and we lose both first
and second things." - C.S. Lewis

My daughter experienced one of the downsides of being a pastor's kid; anything you say can and will be repeated, even if it's supposed to be within a time of "safe" sharing during youth camp. Emily shared something very mild, even a bit humorous, and it only took a few hours for it to travel from youth camp several hundred miles away, to me. She texted me in frustration, and I texted back, "I know it's hard to trust people, but you can trust God, and you can always trust your daddy."

The first chapter of this book described the serious problem of incivility present in the church. But not everyone in the Christian community sees a need for civility when issues of diversity arise that threaten deeply held convictions or preferences. The issues may or may not be essential to Christianity (a distinction made in the next chapter), but they are important nonetheless.

The result is a genuine struggle over the issue of civility by some in the Christian community who see it as an exercise in compromise. To be sure, these are men and women sincerely committed to Jesus, who love the church, the scriptures, and the faith once for all delivered to the saints. That love is expressed in a passionate zeal to contend for and defend the integrity of the faith. Serving, worshipping, and being in relationship with brothers and sisters of this perspective, I believe their intentions to be good, but the lack of civility in how that passion is expressed is not so good.

Out of concern for the nature by which some Christians were engaging the Emerging Church movement, pastor and church planter Jim Belcher sought a conversational approach beyond the unproductive labeling and misrepresentation coming from some Evangelical groups - an approach creating false dichotomies between fellowship and doctrine.

> We place doctrinal purity over unity, or we stress relational purity over sound doctrine. The paradoxical reality is that Jesus wants us to be deeply committed to both-the peace and purity of the church. When this is not the case, our disunity is a major hindrance to our evangelism and witness to the world. We fail at the "final apologetic" our love for one another.[100]

The failure of love results in uncivil disagreements that don't just divide, but destroy, reinforcing a reputation John Stott calls a "pathological tendency to fragment."[101]

Must disagreement be destructive? As long as you and I rub shoulders with each other we will experience conflict, friction, disagreement, and debate. This is inevitable in any relationship and is not necessarily an indicator of incivility. We can disagree passionately yet agreeably, when we understand that our relationship is based on common loyalty and essential unity. In the same way, the church can contend with its members while keeping in mind that we are family. We've been doing it for a long time.

> What we understand so rarely is that the church can have both harmony and love while at the same time having divisions and disagreements. Disagreement does not necessitate disharmony and division need not spawn hatred. Contention can exist within community. It is precisely because people love both the Lord of the church and the church that so much of our ecclesiastical warfare arises.[102]

I think the quote above holds equal parts of the problem and the solution.

Such passionate pursuits of purity by the church insure genuine unity within the church, but unity does not have to mean unison. I love the use of the word *harmony*. There can only be harmony if there are different tones working together. Thus, diversity is essential to the music, even if we have a little trouble getting on key.

In contrast, I find the use of the word *warfare* to be problematic. How can members of one Body, members of a family seeking peace, be at war? Historically, the church's use of culture-war rhetoric might just have us "priming ourselves to view mere critique of Christian principles as personal attack and those who simply disagree with us as hostile adversaries."[103]

When viewed through the lens of warfare, brothers and sisters are mistaken for enemies and often suffer the friendly fire of vilification, and incivility: "Culture-war rhetoric leads us to distort other's positions, to see enmity in place of mere disagreement."[104] Such a posture closes down civil communication rather than encouraging it, resulting in diminishing levels of any positive channel. Family becomes the enemy, and the Body is weaker for it: "By adopting the rhetoric of war, Christians prime themselves to perceive others as 'friend or foe,' and approach complex issues with an either-or mindset."[105]

A clear example of this approach is in the transformation of my own denominational tribe, the Southern Baptist Convention, and in particular, its flagship educational institution, the Southern Baptist Theological Seminary. President, R. Albert Mohler's journey to the leadership and turnover of the seminary involved a strategy that simply eliminated opposition through the severing of personal and professional relationships. Mohler believed "the battle between conservatives and moderates was not a matter of politics or personalities but of presuppositions...these are two fundamentally different understandings of the Baptist faith, Baptist identity, and the future of the SBC."[106]

When he assumed the presidency in 1993, "compromise and accommodation were not strategies he had in mind."[107] Men and women who disagreed with Mohler on women's ordination, young earth creationism, his brand of Calvinism, and other non-essential doctrines were accused of being part of a "moderate, neo-orthodox, liberal bureaucracy."[108] These men and women were dismissed from their denominational and academic responsibilities. Having personally known, read, and studied under some of those dismissed from Southern Seminary I can say that words such as "liberal" and "neo-orthodox" are far from accurate portrayals of their beliefs.

A later example reveals continued misrepresentation and aversion to communication over issues of disagreement. In April of 2012, A Baptist Conference on Sexuality and Covenant was held in Decatur, Georgia. Baptists with various perspectives on sexuality gathered for dialogue, debate, and deeper understanding through worship, prayer, study of scripture, and meaningful conversation. I attended the conference and found much to ponder, much to agree with, and very much to disagree with. Fellow Christians with whom I most strenuously debated have become both very close friends and honest critics. Although I remain committed to a traditional view of marriage (one man and one woman), the conference deepened my understanding on sexuality and my compassion for others whose perspectives I do not embrace. Although my convictions differed from many with whom I engaged, the conversations were civil and very productive.

However, a reporter for *Baptist Press*, the journalism arm of the Southern Baptist Convention, reported,

> Younger Southern Baptists ought to be thankful for being spared such "conversations" and denominational referendums, one in which youthful angst is catapulting the Cooperative Baptist Fellowship to embrace LGBT relations as normative. What I witnessed before the altar of "conversation" was a fellowship cementing its sexual ethics away from Scripture and elevating experience in its place.[109]

Al Mohler, who was not present, stated, "They are making clear decisions to abandon biblical authority in pursuit of endless 'conversations.'"[110] Having attended the event myself, the environment described by the reporter did not resemble what I experienced. Theologian Scot McKnight, while addressing critics of the Emerging Church movement, stressed the importance of fairly and accurately representing the perspectives of those with whom we disagree. He wrote, "We must identify our conversation partners in a way they would recognize."[111] Let me be clear. Andrew Walker is my brother in Christ. He is a thoughtful and talented writer who is passionate in his commitment to seeing God's Word proclaimed. However, from my perspective, Walker's report was an inaccurate and uncivil caricature of the purpose, content and outcome of the conference. There were no denominational referendums, no official embrace of the LGBT lifestyle by the Cooperative Baptist Fellowship, and no effort to abandon biblical authority. Is it not a greater source of concern for the reporter and Mr. Mohler to suggest there be no dialogue between fellow Christ followers?

Sadly, such is the posture of many Christians who confuse unity with uniformity. I've experienced first-hand how it feels to be treated like a heretic over matters of preference, interpretation, and opinion. Such incivility is an attempt to silence voices of civil dissent. However, as John Morley says, "You have not converted a man because you have silenced him." Perhaps my brothers and sisters in the Southern Baptist Convention could gain insight from Tempe, Arizona, Mayor Hugh Hailman, who stated, "Our opponents are not our enemies."[112] Hailman's statement echoes McKnight's caution above. Both Hailman and McKnight's posture toward critics is an invitational one. McKnight called them "conversation partners," a relational term inconsistent with Walker and Mohler's rhetoric of war, exclusivity, and disconnection.[113] A relational approach allows for both unity and diversity to exist in harmony. One can seek to engage in dialogue over controversial matters in a way that honestly addresses points of divergence while keeping the relationship with their "conversation partner" the basis for unity. We have an enemy, a common enemy who I believe is getting abundant satisfaction because of my tribe's penchant for mistaken identity. I am pleading with my Baptist brothers and sisters; stop eating our own. Stop mistaking family for the enemy.

Social critic Os Guinness desires to see civility as the solution to key social issues, and as an example of democracy to other nations. Civility, he writes,

> could be the key to resolving the culture wars, could be a stunning tribute to the brilliance of the 'great experiment' devised by the American founders, and also could stand as an encouragement and as a model for public civility to be considered in other parts of the world.[114]

I contend, however, that for civility to become a value exported by the American people it must have as its foundation an example from the community of faith - a people of grace and truth. What would happen if civility became a major export of Kingdom people to the glocal community?

Summary

Each of the perspectives above represent a small sampling of attempts to address the rise of incivility in the many areas of life we face each day. Each offers a basis related to a belief in how things should be in contrast to how things are. Ethics, morality, sacrifice, productivity, human flourishing, personal gain, altruism, and other motives compel the individual to extend themselves toward others in an effort to create a civil society.

If American civility can contribute to civility elsewhere, if awareness will breed awareness, if civility creates a "ripple effect" as its benefits expand to others,[115] and if civility is morally superior, then why do we still have such a problem?

It's complicated.

A couple years ago my wife was in the car line to pick up our son from elementary school. A guy decided he wanted out of the line, threw his truck in reverse and hit the gas. He crushed the front end of our car then proceeded to try and drive off. An officer witnessed the event and pulled him over. Serena called me and I headed to the school.

My wife and son were fine, so I asked, "Where is the guy?" I looked at his truck, I learned he was uninsured, and the battle began. I know the scriptures instruct us to take every thought captive, but the prison of my mind quickly overcrowded and there was a jailbreak. The officer must have read my expression and the tone of my voice. He held up his hand and said, "Reverend Glenn, please let us handle this." He emphasized *reverend*. I was taken aback. He went on to say that he recognized me from the devotion videos I did for our church's Upward Basketball games where his son played. I immediately apologized and thanked him. He responded by saying that situations like this can easily overwhelm people. "You get flooded, you get angry, and you feel helpless. It's easy to forget who you are and before you know it, you've stooped to the level of the other person." I asked how he and other officers kept their cool. "We're trained to work through a simple process that keeps us focused, in control, and aware of who we are, where we are, and who we represent." He shared the process which was indeed simple, easy to remember, and quickly applicable.

I think that's our problem. The principles in this section are solid, but who can memorize it all? Who can recall it in the heat of the moment? I believe we need a process for choosing civility that is accessible; a process that is at our fingertips in the clutch time of daily life. I know I need it, and the world needs to see it. This book's contribution will include many of the sound principles above, but will present, communicate, apply, and package them in a way that is simple, memorable and portable.

Questions to Ponder

- This chapter is quite candid about the internal conflict within the Body of Christ. How do you respond to Kevin being so direct in his examples

- Discuss the contrast between "family" and "enemy" or "war" language when referring to fellow Christ-followers. Should a brother or sister be treated as an enemy? If so, when?

- How would the "both/and" approach of Polarity Management aid in some of the "either/or" debates addressed in this chapter?

- How do you feel about an ongoing conversation between yourself and another Christian with whom you strongly disagree? Are you engaged in such a relationship? How could such relationships between fellow Christ-followers serve to strengthen our internal fellowship? How would they strengthen our external witness to the world?

- How do you discern between unity and uniformity? Acceptance and affirmation?

- Why do you think John Stott says that Christians have a "pathological tendency to fragment?" What can you do personally to reverse this reality?

- What was the most important takeaway from this chapter for you?

PART 3

The problem addressed in this book is the troubling level of incivility regularly expressed within American culture in general, and within the Christian community in particular. Section one explored several areas where a lack of civility is expressed and experienced in daily life. Among those environments is the Christian community, where a troubling level of incivility is directed by Christians toward other Christians with whom they disagree. Such a practice weakens the unity of the Body of Christ and weakens its witness to the wider culture.

I have seen and continue to witness the devastating effects of the uncivil war taking place within what is supposed to be a community united by faith in a Savior we call the Prince of Peace. The church is called to be countercultural, living in attractional and redemptive contrast to a culture that lives according to the desires of the flesh. We are called to be a peculiar people whose diversity is aligned and arranged according to our essential unity in Christ and His call to unconditional love. Regarding civility, however, the Christian community seems to take its cues from culture rather than running counter to it - pointing out problems in culture while failing to model a better way. Gabe Lyons highlights this trend in his book, *The Next Christians:*

Simply put, relating to the world by following the world can be a recipe for disappointment and disillusionment. Countercultures that point out the problem but offer nothing as a solution ultimately fail in their mission. And pursuing relevance at all costs isn't countercultural at all. The next Christians are living in the tension of being prophetic with their lives while serving others and inviting them to a better way.[116]

How does the church demonstrate that better way, and why? Is civility important to the Body within and to the outside world? Is it necessary, or even wise to practice civility? Isn't civility simply an expression of weakness in one's convictions, or just another way to process a defeatist approach to interaction? How can we practice civility in such a politically, socially, economically, and even theologically polarized culture like that of the U.S.? What role does civility play in the life of a Christ-follower, and is it a role that is profitable or even practical? At the end of the day, is civility a realistic option for Christians?

It is the claim of this book that the Body of Christ can experience greatly improved internal unity, health, morale, stability, as well as a diverse, attractional, educational, and encouraging external witness. This is possible if the church does the following:

- Become aware that civility is a requirement among the Body of Christ.
- Imagine a vision of what a civility-conscious Christian community looks like.
- Embrace the intention to bring such a vision into reality.
- Adopt a posture of learning toward the dynamics of civil communication.
- Apply a practical conversational process that practices civility, essential unity, and mutual respect.

A leading voice in the conversation sees civility as a goal within reach, provided we see it as a discipline requiring work, as an art requiring practice, and as a game to be played.

> The practice of civility is the applying of gentle force with the goal that everybody be a winner in the delicate game of social exchange. As an art, civility has rules one can learn and facility with these rules can improve with practice. This is the good news. The bad news is that often we are unable to imagine the benefits of that learning and practice.[117]

Central to this perspective are elements of decisive action (application of force, practice), imagination (imagine the benefits), and practical tools (rules to learn and facilitate). Each of these three elements is necessary for change to occur. A similar three-fold approach is suggested by the late Christian philosopher Dallas Willard for Christ followers desiring a genuine personal transformation. Willard offers a memorable acronym that captures the importance of each element and its necessity for real change: "To keep the general pattern in mind, we will use the acronym, 'VIM.' As in the phrase 'vim and vigor.' 'Vim' is a derivative of the Latin term *vis* meaning direction, strength, force, vigor, power, energy, or virtue."[118] Willard's acronym "VIM" stands for Vision, Intention, and Means, and will guide our continued journey.

Vision refers to what is seen in the gap between what is and what could, should, or ought to be. It is the imaginative element necessary to begin our transformation. *Intention* refers to the deliberate decision and commitment to bring the vision into reality by putting thoughts into action. *Means* are the practical steps, tools, skill, or processes by which the intentions are implemented. All three are interdependent and necessary to accomplish the renovation of civility for the Christian community.

CHAPTER 9

Vision

*"Hope has 2 beautiful daughters: Anger and Courage.
Anger at the way things are. Courage to ensure
they don't stay that way" -St. Augustine*

*"Where there is no vision, there is no hope."-
George Washington Carver*

To a large degree, Jesus has already provided the vision for unity and civility. Shortly before his passion, Jesus prays that his followers, present and future, would "all be one." In the same discourse, Christian unity provides the strength for believers to be in the world, but not of the world. It is in our loving unity that Jesus says "the world will know that you are my disciples."[119] Such a clear and compelling vision set forth by Jesus himself would surely provide enough to get the church started toward the realization of a civility-conscious vision. However, it is often hard for people, even Christians, to imagine civility as a beneficial endeavor. Perspectives can be skewed by false and fuzzy perceptions of what such a reality would and would not look like. The following section addresses common misconceptions regarding civility by examining what civility is not.

What Civility Is Not

Civility is not the absence of conflict. In a series on marriage, I prepared an entire sermon on the reality of conflict in marriage and principles for couples to approach their disagreements with civility. A couple approached me after the service. The husband was most upset that I would "endorse" conflict in a marriage.

For him, an ideal Christian marriage should be one that resembled his own: a relationship free of conflict. He went on to claim that they had enjoyed more than 15 years of marriage without a single argument. Of course, the husband did all of the talking. Come to think of it, I don't believe I have ever heard his wife speak.

The interaction raises a common misperception about civility. Does a vision of Christian civility demand the absence of any conflict? Is it somehow uncivil to disagree at all, to hold convictions, and to passionately articulate and defend to convictions?

Blogger, author, and Bible teacher Frank Viola writes, "Civil disagreement and even debate, when done in the spirit of Christ, are healthy and helpful."[120] The two terms *healthy* and *conflict* may sound like an oxymoron. Wouldn't healthy relationships be characterized by avoidance of conflict? The answer depends on what you think of when hearing the word, conflict. Communication scholars report most people share words like *war, hate, battle, failure, anger, lose,* and *argue,* when associated with the term *conflict.*

Semiotically, "conflict" conjures negative metaphors, collateral images, and experiences. Therefore, it is naturally avoided.[121] However, the Christian community can imagine a better way regarding conflict, seeing it as redemptive, productive, and instructional.

It is often the very resistance brought on by healthy conflict that cause relationships to deepen in trust. Conflict among fully engaged individuals is a catalyst to growth. Pastor and church consultant Mel Lawrenz imagines civility through the idea of engagement. In his vision, Christ followers remain consistently engaged with God, one another, their community, and their world. As such they are in a consistent position to establish and maintain healthy relational connections.[122] However, Lawrenz recognizes that such relational connections are not free from conflict, for the connections are between human beings. "Conflict is inevitable as long as we are human. The questions become how to lessen the frequency of conflict and how to deal constructively with conflict when it does arise."[123] Communication professors Tim Muehlhoff and Todd Lewis remind Christ-followers, "Conflict is common, and in a sense inevitable to all relationships."[124] The tension present within relationships of inevitable conflict helps us keep in mind that civility is in the best sense of the word, "practiced."[125]

Practicing conflict is hardly a new concept for the followers of Jesus. The early church was not a sanitized, conflict-free environment. Jesus was in constant conflict with the religious leaders of his day and led a band of constantly squabbling disciples.[126] Paul confronts Peter publicly over his uncivil table manners toward Gentile believers.[127] The Jewish church was deeply and passionately divided over whether or not to recognize Gentile converts to the Way.[128] Paul played referee to warring factions in Corinth, and pled with two women in Philippi who could agree on nothing else, to "agree in the Lord."[129]

The community of the Prince of Peace has been a laboratory of civil conflict since the beginning. Yet as much as they zealously debated their differences, their practiced goals were to pursue Shalom between one another for the sake of Christ's gospel of peace. Civility calls believers to the gymnasium of grace to wrestle vigorously with their differences. Civility also calls us to the laboratory of love wherein our diversity is contended, tested, and our conflicts seek to be resolved. The Christ-follower can emerge with greater strength, depth of character, and a clear perception of what it means to choose civility.

Civility is not the absence of conviction. In April of 1862, Ralph Waldo Emerson wrote an essay for *The Atlantic* magazine. In it, he praised President Lincoln for his resolve in seeking to emancipate slaves; an action perceived by many in the south as a threat to their established civilization. Emerson observed that America was attempting

> to hold together two states of civilization: a higher state, where labor and the tenure of land and the right of suffrage are democratic; and a lower state, in which the old military tenure of prisoners or slaves, and of power and land in a few hands, makes an oligarchy: we have attempted to hold these two states of society under one law. But the rude and early state of society does not work well with the later, nay, works badly, and has poisoned politics, public morals, and social intercourse in the Republic, now for many years.[130]

Emerson continued, asking, "should not the best civilization be extended over the whole country, since the disorder of the less civilized portion menaces the existence of the country?"[131] Emerson's polished yet passionate plea is grounded in his belief that true civility is connected to firm convictions. "There can be no high civility without a deep morality."[132] Pulitzer Prize winning journalist J. Anthony Lukas stated his belief that the moral decline in his city is realized because "we have let our standards of civility and truth waste dangerously away."[133] Emerson and Lukas each in their own way convey an approach to civility that is essentially connected to conviction. It is the reversal of what W.B. Yeats describes in his poem, "Second Coming,": "The best lack all conviction while the worst are full of passionate intensity."[134] Such a reversal is needed, for the concern of some is that along with civility comes passionless indifference, or even a posture of compromise. Lutheran pastor and scholar Martin Marty framed the concern as follows; "people who are good at being civil often lack strong convictions, and people with strong convictions often lack civility."[135] If we desire to be more civil, however, it need not be at the expense of our convictions. Richard

Mouw, quoting the late Martin E. Marty, calls this "convicted civility."[136]

Expressing civility does not mean we're prohibited from prophetic criticism of the thinking, beliefs, behaviors, and other systemic realities of the times. While it may be true that civility calls for us to affirm the right of another to express their beliefs, civility does not demand that we accept, affirm, or approve of those beliefs and their resulting actions. Saying one has the right to express their convictions is one thing; saying they are right in how they express them is something different. Civil conviction calls us to the former, not the latter.

Is a convicted civility judgmental? What about judging others? How does a civil conviction avoid the "judgmental" label?

The idea of a truly non-judgmental posture is unrealistic. To say one should not be judgmental is itself a judgmental statement. As volitional beings, humans make decisions based on judgments toward the value of options from which they choose. There are differing value systems, and those values come into conflict requiring one to judge between which values to adopt. To become non-judgmental is to stop thinking. It cannot be done.

The concept of judgment is greatly misunderstood. The scriptures instruct Christ- followers to make wise judgments regarding what is true and what is good (Isaiah 5:20, Matthew 7:15-19, Galatians 5:16-23), yet according to Paul Copan, the most frequently quoted verse in the Bible is Matthew 7:1, "Do not judge, or you too will be judged."[137] A vision for civility grounded in Christian conviction will be fuzzy at best without clarity on this issue.

Jesus' instructions here are not a blanket disregard for probing investigation, insightful evaluation, critical thinking, wise discernment, or perceptive decision making. Jesus is waving a caution flag against a particular sort of judgmental attitude - self-righteousness. In Matthew 7:1-5, Jesus was condemning those who judge using two standards of morality; one standard for themselves and another for the one they accuse.

Luke 6:37-38 also condemns a self-righteous attitude. Michael Card observes this as the connection between both passages; "A judgmental attitude inevitably leads to a harshness of spirit that renders a person unable to [give or] receive forgiveness."[138]

How then did Jesus respond to those living according to beliefs contrary to the Father's will? How did Jesus model "judgment" that accepted and affirmed people while not approving or affirming their sin? What qualifies a civility that connects conviction *and* compassion?

When the gospel narratives describe Jesus "accepting" prostitutes, tax collectors, and others considered sinful, there is no indication he accepted their *behaviors*. He called Matthew to follow him (requiring Matthew to leave behind his previous life), he called the woman at the well to forsake her lifestyle of promiscuity, he called the woman caught in adultery to leave her life of sin, and he called Zacchaeus to redemptive restitution. "Jesus refused to define people in terms of their present sordid circumstances. He affirmed their *potential* for living as faithful and creative children of God."[139]

This is no doubt a difficult position for Christ-followers to take, but one that the church is called to nonetheless,

> It has never been easy for the church to nurture a convicted civility. Indeed, when the biblical writer first urged the followers of Christ to 'pursue peace with everyone,' the society was at least as multicultural and pluralistic as today ... If they could work at treating people with gentleness and reverence in such an environment, what is our excuse for attempting less?[140]

Civility is not exclusive to evangelism. Because a diminished Christian witness as a result of incivility is part of the motivation for this book, it does not follow that civility be expressed only as a means to achieve an evangelistic conversation. I know that civility will play an important part in establishing a relationship that earns us the right to share our faith with others (I've never seen rudeness lead to redemption). However, if kindness and gentleness are only expressed as means to conversion, one could argue that civility becomes a manipulative tool for proselytizing, not an expression of genuine interest and respect in pursuit of a relationship.

No one enjoys being objectified as a project, conquest, or otherwise proverbial notch on someone's belt. However, when we are the subject of another's thoughts, interest or admiration, a relationship is formed that over time may deepen in trust and security. Leonard Sweet describes this process in the following way: "Objectivity becomes subjectivity because of relativity."[141] Civility's role in evangelism is important as long as the relationship is pursued out of interest in the individual as a subject of mutual respect, and not out of interest in the individual as a statistical object.

Civility does not demand we prefer the company of everyone to whom we are civil. The research done in preparation for this book yielded a surprising discovery. People commonly assumed being civil meant becoming friends. Naturally the question arose, "Do we have to be civil if we don't want to be their friend?"

This requires a confession and a concession on my part. I confess that while I love my church family and would be there to support and help any of them, there are some of them who simply irritate me. To be fair, I am certain I irritate some of them as well!! Therefore, I concede that while civility has great potential for positive Christian witness, redemptive communication, and improved health within the family of faith, the downside is that we cannot always pick our relatives. As a result, this process has the potential to galvanize non-essential differences to the degree that while we understand the need to respect each other, seek to understand each other, and work to love each other, there is no guarantee it will make us like each other.

Furthermore, civility is not limited to those we know. Because the word describes what is good for "the city," it carries the notion that civility will be expressed to strangers with whom we have little connection. In this way, civility contains elements of fellowship, wherein we are civil to those we know, as well as elements of hospitality, wherein we extend gentleness and respect to strangers. While it may indeed be optional to prefer someone's company, to be kind, gentle, and hospitable are expressions required for followers of Jesus. Christine Pohl offers a compelling summary:

> Hospitality is not optional for Christians, nor is it limited to those who are especially gifted for it. It is, instead, a necessary practice in the community of faith. One of the key Greek words for hospitality, *philoxenia,* combines the general word for love or affection for people who are connected by kinship or faith *(phileo),* and the word for stranger *(xenos).* Thus etymologically and practically, in the New Testament, hospitality is closely connected to love. Because *philoxenia* includes the word for strangers, hospitality's orientation toward strangers is also more apparent in Greek than in English.[142]

While we are not required to like everyone, we are expected to express love to each other, whether brother, sister, friend, opponent, or stranger.

Having clarified several important and potential misconceptions regarding civility, the next section seeks to bring a vision for civility into sharper focus by analyzing important defining elements of Christian civility.

What Civility Will Require

Section two demonstrated that civility is comprised of various elements, is informed by various disciplines, and is expressed through a diversity of communication mediums and opportunities. Followers of Jesus encounter opportunities each day to express civility when commenting on a friend's Facebook status, when expressing concern over poor customer service to a manager, when receiving constructive criticism from a supervisor, or when enduring an irrational tirade from a fellow Christian over a political issue. In each situation we get to *choose* how to respond.

Stephen Carter bases one's decision on a moral mandate, and Richard Mouw points to civility as a sign of spiritual maturity. Civility, therefore, can be understood as "public politeness": a kindness, gentleness, and meekness expressed in diversely united community. Meekness is an important description, as it describes not weakness, as many believe, but instead a passion or power under control. Aristotle, in fact, taught meekness as the middle ground between excessive anger and excessive lack of anger.[143] It is a quiet strength.

What does this convicted, compassionate civility look like? On what principles can the diverse members of the Body of Christ find harmony? What determines whether these differing notes remain dissonant or resolve to harmony? There are three particular recognitions necessary to achieve such a relationally harmonious approach.

Recognize that error is more a path to growth than it is a slippery slope toward apostasy. Believers can temper their fear of error by understanding error to be what makes one truly human, as Augustine writes, "*fallor ergo sum*: I err, therefore, I am."[144] Once, at a T-ball game with my son, I observed signs with bold red letters that warned, "Do not yell at the umpires. Nobody's perfect, not even YOU!" Error is common to humanity. Yet, it's natural to read the previous statement and think of someone else rather than yourself. Instead, what if you and I looked in the mirror instead of looking through the window? It is difficult to embrace the vibrancy of faith, to be relationally present, and to express civility within the tensions of life until we are set free from the fear of error. In her book,

Being Wrong: Adventures in the Margin of Error, journalist, Kathryn Schultz writes,

> Far from being a moral flaw, [error] is inextricable from some of our most humane and honorable qualities: empathy, optimism, imagination, conviction, and courage. And far from being a mark of indifference or intolerance, wrongness is a vital part of how we learn and change ... it is ultimately wrongness, not rightness that can teach us who we are.[145]

Recognize how wide a platform exists for unity among Christians. It is troubling the speed at which individuals will simply dismiss one with views contrary to their perceived set of non-negotiable beliefs.[146]

Pastor and author David Platt shared that on any controversial issue there are ditches on both sides that one can fall into. Between those ditches is a wide road, "when someone has fallen into one ditch, it's silly to assume that by attempting to climb out of that ditch, they are doomed to slide into the other."[147] The wide road in between is where one encounters people who travel from both sides of an issue. It's where the tension may be tangible, but perhaps it's where the music of grace is most vibrant. Music producer Roy Salmond's church included a call for "vibrant faith" in its mission statement. He immediately connected vibrancy with vibration. He visualized the tension present in a guitar string stretched between two fixed points. "A vibrant faith," he cautioned his church "may necessitate oscillation and tension. In the absence of motion, [however], there's no music."[148] As stated above, it is the fear of being rejected at the base of our identity that causes many to simply hold fast to one pole of tension at the rejection of the other instead of seeking ways to embrace the tension at both ends. Perhaps a way forward is found in the lyrics of an old hymn entitled, *There's A Wideness in God's Mercy.*

There's a wideness in God's mercy, like the wideness
of the sea;
There's a kindness in His justice, which is more
than liberty.
For the love of God is broader than the measure of
our mind;
And the heart of the Eternal is most wonderfully
kind.
But we make His love too narrow by false limits of
our own;
And we magnify His strictness with a zeal He will
not own.[149]

Just as the fear of being wrong can be overcome through a
realization of error's role in maturity, we can also embrace the
vibrancy of tension through an understanding of how robust and
encompassing God's mercy is. This in no way suggests the absence
non-negotiable beliefs in the Christian faith. Such beliefs are made
clear in the witness of scripture, held consistently within the corpus
of teaching by the church fathers, and encapsulated in the Creeds.
However, it is suggested here that followers of Jesus have a tendency
to place an increasing number of non-essentials on the essentials
list, overlooking the reality that there exist far fewer issues for which
there must be a clear resolution than there are issues that allow for
vibrancy and civil dialogue.

**Recognize the strength of the Body's unity is the sum of its
diversity.** C.S. Lewis described the essentials as "Mere Christianity,"
and went on to provide a verbal image in the form of a great hallway
containing doors that open to several rooms. He sees the hallway
itself as a place of commonality, but understands the exclusivity of
some issues will not permit believers to enter all the rooms together.
"If I can bring anyone into that hall I shall have done what I
attempted. But it is in the rooms, not in the hall, that there are fires

and chairs and meals."[150] What Lewis describes as halls and rooms, Jim Belcher describes as tiers:

> I look at it in tiers. The first tier is the important things such as what we believe about God, Christ, etc. The second, while still important is not as crucial and usually includes things like denominational distinctions. And third tier includes even lesser important things. The church of mere Christians is a hallway with many different rooms, but one hallway. [151]

This approach is echoed by R. Albert Mohler, president of the Southern Baptist Theological Seminary, who uses the term *order* rather than *tiers*. Nevertheless, like Belcher, Mohler understands first-order theological issues to include doctrines central to the Christian faith such as the Trinity, the deity and humanity of Jesus, justification by faith, and the authority of Scripture. According to Mohler, "These first-order doctrines represent the most fundamental truths of the Christian faith, and a denial of these doctrines represents nothing less than an eventual denial of Christianity itself."[152] For Mohler, second-order doctrines allow believing Christians to disagree on certain issues, but such disagreement may create significant boundaries between believers. Third-order issues allow Christians to disagree and remain in close fellowship.[153]

I would question the need for three categories, believing the unnecessary distinction between second and third tier/order minimizes the concept of things indifferent, or "adiaphora." These are issues that while important and certainly debatable are indifferent to salvation.[154] In addition, the second/third tier distinction enables what Robert Greer calls "denominational chauvinism,"[155] wherein a group is able to affirm unity in Jesus but still maintain denominationally exclusive interaction. I contend such deliberate and unnecessary exclusivity does not strengthen those members who withdraw to their own "rooms" (to use Lewis' metaphor), but it simply creates an echo chamber that weakens both their ability to interact with the wider Christian community, and even more with the outside world. Best-selling author Steven Johnson describes the weakening effects of the echo-chamber:

> When groups can filter their news by ideological persuasion, the long-term tendency is toward increased polarization and decreased consensus. Individuals' interpretation of the world get amplified and not challenged; the common ground of social agreement shrinks. When groups are exposed to a more diverse range of perspectives, when their values are forced to confront different viewpoints, they are likely to approach the world in a more nuanced way, and avoid falling prey to crude extremism.[156]

Johnson supports this statement by citing longitudinal studies from University of Michigan professor Scott E. Page, developer of the "Diversity Trumps Homogeneity Theorem."[157] For over 20 years, Page grouped test subjects based on homogenous skill, perspective, and I.Q. over against groups scoring slightly lower in I.Q. tests, but diverse in their range of skill, profession, and perspective. Page consistently found that diverse groups were collectively smarter and more effective at problem solving than the homogenous groups. If civility can diminish the partitions built over non-essential issues I am convinced a stronger, smarter, and more robust Body could emerge. Civility is necessary to understand that united diversity matters more than compartmentalized denominational exclusivity.

Although denominational chauvinism remains alive and well in the Christian community, perhaps the similar definitions of first order issues from C.S. Lewis, an Anglican layman; Belcher, an Emergent Church planter; and Mohler, a Southern Baptist, offer a hopeful if not accidental demonstration of diverse unity. Such a unity is built on the notion that while essential issues are clear, they are also few. Therefore, plenty of room is present for Christ-followers to confidently embrace the vibrancy found in non-essential issues, while standing united in Christ as a force for good. Such an understanding of what is essential and non-essential will allow the Christian community to model for one another, and to the watching world, a realized vision for convicted and compassionate civility – a civility expressed within a community at its best when its diverse members find unity and strength in the One they value most.

Questions to Ponder

- How do you process the idea of "healthy conflict?" How might Proverbs 27:17 provide a helpful way to understanding and explaining a constructive approach to conflict.

- Discuss Kevin's suggestion that civility does not demand the absence of conflict and/or conviction. How has this changed or challenged your understanding of civility?

- How much does the fear of being wrong play in to your conversational approach? In what ways has being corrected helped you learn and grow? How does *fallor ergo sum* help?

- How could civility allow you to hold in tension your convictions along with the possibility of being wrong?

- Talk about what you believe to be the essentials (first order/tier) issues of faith. What are the non-essentials? How is your list different from others of like faith? As a group, talk through these differences. Are some non-essentials elevated? Are some essentials compromised? Can you find more room for unity than for disunity? How?

- Regarding non-essentials, do you see a need for three levels? Do you agree with Kevin that non-essentials should not divide fellowship? Why or why not?

- What are your thoughts on applying the "Diversity Trumps Homogeneity Theorem" to the Body of Christ?

- What was the most important takeaway from this chapter for you?

CHAPTER 10

Intention

"Let us not be content to wait and see what will happen, but give us the determination to make the right things happen." - Horace Mann

"All great acts are ruled by intention. What you mean is what you get." - Brenna Yovanoff

With a clarified vision for civility presented, the opportunity before the Christ follower will proceed only as far as they intend to bring the vision into reality. But what forms the basis of motivation for a follower of Christ to embrace this vision?

The gospel of grace is the crown jewel into which the light of Christ's unconditional love is radiated to one another and to the world that lives in darkness. The light is reflected from its single source, Christ the Lord. However, that single source of light is also refracted, displaying a rainbow of vivid colors - differences arising from the multi-faceted perspectives, personalities, contexts, experiences, and other sources of variation "cut" into the jewel. Same diamond, single source of light, united reflection, diverse refraction.

The Body's incivility has diminished the brilliance of the reflection and muted its colorful refraction. The darkened result casts more shadow than light, failing to provide illumination to those within the Body and to those outside. If the church is no brighter than the world, how can its internal interaction and external witness shed any light on the problem? It is the bond of love that holds together the diverse pieces of Christ's church, creating in mosaic form the image of the church's Master Artisan. New Testament scholar Merrill Tenney offers a compelling observation of this principle in relation to the patchwork of personalities forming Jesus' original disciples,

> "The attitude of love would be the bind that would keep them united and would be the convincing demonstration that they had partaken if his own spirit and purpose."[158]

Pursue civility as a facet of discipleship. Like others referenced thus far, Richard Mouw confirms the damage of incivility to relationships, education, politics, and the business world. However, Mouw takes the conversation further. He claims Christian civility is an issue of discipleship, conviction, and obedience to the way and witness of Jesus.

> We were created for kind and gentle living. Indeed, kindness and gentleness are two of the fruit-of-the-Spirit characteristics that the apostle Paul mentions in Galatians 5. When Christians fail to measure up to the standards of kindness and gentleness, we are not the people God meant us to be.[159]

Gary Kinnaman echoes the same sentiment: "I believe that now more than ever, the world needs the church to be the people of God, like Jesus, full of truth and grace. People who know what they believe and where they stand, but who have the depth of character to speak the truth in love."[160]

The Christ-follower's diligent pursuit of relational unity within a framework of love is a primary identifier of one's devotion to the way of Jesus. Equal to this is the diligence of Christ-followers to seek civil and reasonable resolution to interpersonal conflicts that pose a threat to the Body's unity and bond of love. "Even if believers cannot fully resolve their differences, how can conflict be managed in a way that our witness is preserved? In light of Christ's command all believers have a vested interest in learning how to understand and resolve conflict."[161]

Seeing no exemptions and no exceptions to this rule of love, I have come to understand civility to be a foundational virtue for the advancement of human flourishing in general, and an essential expression of engagement within the Body of Christ in particular. For every Christ follower, civility is an expression of grace needed by the believer, an expression to be expected in a Christian's interactions with fellow believers, and an expression essential for the witness of the gospel's message of grace to the watching world. As James Davidson Hunter observes, "If Christians cannot extend grace through faithful presence within the body of believers, they will not be able to extend grace to those outside."[162]

Become a student of communication. No doubt, every Christian that chooses to make civility their intention will need prayer, the study of scripture, and reliance on the Holy Spirit. Such an intention can be daunting, in light of how deeply seated incivility has become, even in the church. Muehlhoff and Lewis, communication professors by trade acknowledge the intimidation factor.

> God has entrusted his gospel to human communicators and asked that it be taken to all people. As followers of Christ, how are we to accomplish these daunting commands? Part of the answer will be constant reliance on the Holy Spirit, prayer and a deep understanding of the scriptures. However, it will also require each of us to become students of communication. What unifies each biblical command is that communication skills are necessary to fulfill them.[163]

An important realization before pursuing civility is the humility to realize how little one understands communication. Seeing ourselves as students of communication has the potential to keep us aware of the need to practice what we learn, and aware that there is always more to learn. Because incivility typically surfaces within an environment of conflict or tension, understanding how words work and how communication carries deep meaning can allow believers to create the environment Jesus envisioned for his peace-making people.

Section two demonstrated a thumbnail sketch of the many resources available for helping people address conflict, bullying, workplace hostility, online trolling, and other forms of incivility. What is needed for followers of Jesus committed to civility is the creation and compilation of information gathered, analyzed, synthesized, understood, and applied to the problem of incivility.

Imagine a deliberate grassroots effort by Christians to become conversant in basic communication approaches, conflict resolution, polarity management, semiotics, and other ways by which those who worship the incarnate Word would become students of how his words and ways can become embodied in ours. Such a movement would require the participation of churches since Christians committed to civility will need a place to practice. While the church is part of the problem currently, the church is uniquely positioned, gifted, and called to become the epicenter of the solution.

Encourage churches to become spaces for experimenting, training, and practicing civility. In order for civility to move from private endeavor to public reality, the application and practice of what one learns as a student of communication will need to be tested, tried, tweaked, and taught to other believers. Just as the problem of civility in the church is not a private matter, the righteousness of civility is not a private matter. The lessons and life change toward civility are intentions that cannot be kept to ourselves.

The Body needs its fellow members in order to become healthy. Therefore, I believe the local church is the primary catalyst for encouraging, equipping, enabling, and engaging Christians in the application and practice of civility. Richard Mouw writes, "The church is the primary context for learning public righteousness. This means our message to the larger society will be credible only if we can invite others to be more like us."[164] Unless the church's execution of civility is polished, effective, and attractive, why would the world be at all curious, let alone captivated? To accomplish this, Christians will need a great deal of practice.

In his first letter to Timothy, Paul writes, "Have nothing to do with godless myths and old wives' tales; rather, train yourself to be godly. For physical training is of some value, but godliness has value for all things, holding promise for both the present life and the life to come."[165] The passage is often applied using the metaphor of a "gymnasium of the soul,"[166] and is consistent with Leonard Sweet's concept of "practicing," or even "playing," in order to become better at our expressions of righteousness.[167]

Whether churches open their doors to the public as a "Third Space,"[168] create such a space outside their walls, or whether believers gather in private for the purpose of working out their practices of civility, the church as people scattered or in a place gathered can endeavor to be "caught" practicing civility toward one another by a world searching for such a community.

Questions to Ponder

- Chapter 10 claimed that civility is connected to hospitality. In this chapter, the importance of civility is raised as a part of discipleship. How do you respond to this claim?
- Discuss the implications of civility as an expectation and indication of Christian maturity. How does this change the value of civility in your mind? What role must cultivating civility now play in the process of Christian education, spiritual formation, or other forms of ministry?
- Brainstorm with your group some ways to become a student of communication. Check the bibliography for this chapter for helpful resources. What proactive approaches could be taken? What areas of communication would you personally benefit from most?
- To what extent can your own church become a "laboratory" for discovering, training, practicing, and modeling civility? What would this look like? What would keep your worship community from becoming such a place?
- If you are a leader, talk with your staff about ways to create, discover, acquire, or otherwise include tangible teaching on communication and civility in your Church programming. Pastors, how can you and your staff teach, preach, promote, and be "caught" as examples of convicted, compassionate civil communication?
- How would an understanding in communication and civility help you to interact with those of different perspectives?
- What was the most important takeaway from this chapter for you?

CHAPTER 11

Means

"I cannot say whether things will get better if we change; what I can say is that they must change if they are to get better." - Georg C. Lichtenberg

Peace is not merely a distant goal that we seek, but a means by which we arrive at that goal. – Dr. Martin Luther King Jr.

In order for vision and intention to become actual expressions of civility, we need the means to bring what has been dreamed and decided into demonstrable practice. This requires goals that are tangible, settings that are acceptable, steps that are repeatable, and a conversational process that is simple, practical, memorable, and portable.

Set Tangible Goals

Relational communication scholars William Wilmot and Joyce Hockner describe four goals essential to productive and civil interpersonal conversations over issues of conflict.[169]

Content goals. Also known as "topic goals," this involves working to establish a shared goal for what will be accomplished through the conversation. Leadership expert Stephen Covey calls this the principle of "beginning with the end in mind."[170]

Relational goals. These goals involve the type of relationship participants want to maintain during the conflict. Since the focus of this book is on civility in the church, a foundational goal is for participants to relate to one another as brothers and sisters in Christ. Even if the parties see one another as opponents, "our opponents are not our enemies."[171]

Identity goals. Somewhat similar to relational goals, identity goals establish how each party wants to be viewed by the other. In a variation of the Golden Rule, each party is in the position to model the attitude and behavior consistent with how they want to be viewed by the other.

Process goals. Given the first three goals are set, this goal determines the process by which the communication will progress. Will the dialogue take place in person, via email, one-on one, with a facilitator, etc.?

Because the work involved in establishing tangible goals requires a certain level of civility, it is possible for these preliminary exercise to resolve the conflict altogether. If the conversations require additional engagement, it is important to have the means to create the best possible setting for the dialogue to take place.

Create safe settings

Marital therapist John Gottman is able to predict with startling accuracy the outcome of a conversation between people within the first three minutes. The secret, while insightful, is simple, and entirely within one's control. According to Gottman, it's all in how the conversation is set up by one's body language and vocal intensity; actions, if expressed with the gentleness, respect, and restraint that define civility, can almost guarantee a productive conversation.

Turn toward and start soft. Gottman's tools for conversational kick-starts have benefitted thousands of people over his career as a therapist. He suggests the physical posture of turning one's body toward their conversation partner and maintaining an open position: arms not crossed in front or behind, nor hands in pockets. One's palms should be open (this is not one of Gottman's suggestions, but will be explained later). If it is possible to sit across from the person, do so. Lean forward and look in the face, making appropriate eye contact, but not constant eye contact. The position is strong, but invitational.

Vocally, begin the conversation with a choice of words and volume that is not harsh. If the other person begins harshly, do not respond in kind. Gottman believes a "soft start up" is even more important than turning toward, but both are effective tools. Several thousand years before John Gottman called for this approach, the wisdom literature of the Old Testament observed, "A gentle answer turns away wrath, but a harsh word stirs up anger."[172]

The research of Jack Gibb reveals six forms of communication that create a defensive conversational setting and six that create a supportive and productive setting.[173] He lists the forms in contrasting pairs. For purposes of simplicity, I'm interpreting Gibb's list with six positive principles.

Describe my side. When our thoughts are too quickly evaluated or analyzed, it becomes very easy to get defensive. In contrast, working to describe the other's concerns or feelings is validating and aids in understanding the nature of the issue in dispute.

Dare to care. Progress is stalled when our concerns are met with a detached and stoic response. In contrast, an empathetic acknowledgement provides a tone of understanding and invites further openness. Keep in mind that the opposite of love is not hate, it's apathy. We are most like Jesus in our response when we express our compassion through empathy.

Converse, don't compete. When dialogue gives way to responses that sound strategic, scripted, or intended to score debate points, the setting will devolve. Listen and respond, but not in a manner that appears to be competitive. How do you know if you're really listening? Are you hearing the concerns and taking time to process a response, or are you busy think of what to say next? My grandmother used to tell me, "Kevin, quit talkin' in your head and listen to me."

Think with me, not for me. Such a setting can be detected when one party attempts to manipulate and coerce the other to adopt their view. It can become a form of relational bullying. In contrast, civil conversations seek collaboration, with all parties working together toward resolution.

Reserve the right to be wrong. Language loaded with dogmatism is a descriptor of this setting. There is little progress when one believes their views to be absolute. On the other hand, blogger Brian Konkol suggests "a true and genuine dialogue only takes place when a person is willing to be 'converted' to the other side of the argument." At first pass, the statement caused me to become defensive, but once again I could hear the wise voice of my grandmother, "Kevin, you'll learn in life that some people don't want to be confused with the facts since their minds are already made up." I think my Granny was on to something. When we enter a conversation with a teachable spirit, even in passionate disagreement, we are able to learn and better understand. Jim Belcher expands on a conversational posture he learned from Richard Mouw, called "cognitive modesty":

> This does not mean we are not confident in what we know by faith but that we are modest and humble in how we communicate what we know and we do so with a teachable spirit that communicates that we may be wrong on some issues and are open to learning and growing.[174]

Cognitive modesty does not mean that I sacrifice my convictions or tell people what they want to hear. It means that I recognize the limitations of what I know, what I understand, and what I've experienced. I listen closely to others in the conversation with the intention of expanding those limits, deepening my understanding, correcting my misunderstanding, and gaining insight from another's experience. It does not mean that I come to agree with them. It does mean that I am modest enough to take seriously what I can learn, and how I can better communicate about the issue, whether I am compelled to change my mind or not.

Talk with me, not at me. Civility is difficult if one behaves as though they are superior to the other. A posture of equality creates a setting more likely to result in progress toward resolution.

Central to each of the settings above is the simple, but essential quality of treating the other as one created in the image of God, and therefore deserving of respect, even if for their potential. Followers of Jesus can create climates of civility within which problems, issues, questions, tensions, and other forms of conflict can be addressed. Such climate control is determined by "the degree to which people see themselves as valued."[175]

Prepare the heart for civil engagement.

> No spirituality of civility is adequate without self - critique - taking an honest look at our own motives and purposes. And this can only happen when we acknowledge that we desperately need God to reveal to us what is really going on in our inner being.[176]

Biblical scholar Richard Pratt describes his experience viewing a stained glass window. Looking through the glass, he observed the passing clouds outside. When the light shifted, he saw his reflection in the glass, like a mirror. Finally, he saw the artistic image, the picture itself. He compared the experience to what it means for one to truly encounter the Lord through the scriptures: a mirror by which we see ourselves, a window through which we see the world, and an image in which we come face to face with the story and its Author.[177]

The following questions are helpful means for one's practice of self-critique. As the questions become more familiar, they can become a repeatable series of filters or steps to clarify the effect an issue of conflict is having on one's self, and thus assist us in responding to conflict versus reacting to it.

What exactly set off the conflict? Think through the source of the problem for accurate assessment. What was my contribution to the source of this conflict, if any?

How do I understand the conflict? Can I describe what the conflict is about? Many disputes become much worse because of misunderstandings leading to misrepresentations, and so on. Seek to clearly understand the conflict.

What are they seeing? This is an instance where familiarity with semiotics, particularly familiarity with collateral experience, is helpful for understanding what the source of the conflict signifies for others involved. Such insight can allow us to respond with sensitivity and helpful understanding as communication is adjusted to account for the collateral experience encountered: "All of us need to become adept translators of the symbols we use on a daily basis."[178]

What is this doing in me? This is a deep level of honesty, and requires maturity. Is the conflict provoking you in a way that is disproportionate to its source? What emotions, feelings, memories, or other responses is the conflict raising in you? Are your responses such that you can effectively address the conflict, or do you need assistance, time to process, or to establish a boundary?

What is causing this inner struggle in me? Do you have your own collateral experience that makes you more or less able to respond with civility to this conflict? Would sharing such information make the setting more or less positive and productive?

It is clear that followers of Jesus, while pursuing civility, are nonetheless products of dysfunction, brokenness, and our own insecurities. Civility is hard work requiring training, practice, and honest self-appraisal, and perhaps time and distance before we are prepared to address the conflict in a civil manner.

Civility is a descriptive quality of a follower of Jesus; therefore, it requires that each one turn to Christ in preparation for a life of civility that embodies the truth of Jesus in its conviction, the grace of Jesus in its compassion, and the way of Jesus in its expression.

Questions to Ponder

- How did the information in this chapter help with the practical nature of preparing yourself for civil discourse?
- Which tools did you find to be the most natural? Which ones do you find challenging?
- What other insights, actions, or experiences would you add to this chapter? Share those with the discussion group.
- Discuss the importance of the self-critique exercise. What would this be a beneficial form of evaluation before and after a confrontation?
- Kevin references lessons from his Grandmother quite a bit (listening to a few of his sermons will reveal even more valuable insights from "Granny"). Are there people in your life from whom you've learned such wisdom up close? Talk about those relationships and lessons. How do you process the idea that you can have such an influence on the next generation? What sort of wisdom do you want to be remembered for?
- What was the most important takeaway from this chapter for you?

CHAPTER 12

Palms Up

*"I used to think clenched fists would help me fight better,
but now I know they make me weaker." – Bob Goff*

Throughout this journey together, I've attempted to draw attention to the problem of incivility within the Christian community in contrast to Jesus' call and command to his followers that their words and ways reflect the sacrificial, convicted, and compassionate civility he modeled. Civility works to build a diverse unity within the Body of Christ, modeling to the searching and watching world a way of living, moving and having our being within a community dedicated to the pursuit of both individual and collective human flourishing. In a word, *shalom*. Theologian Cornelius Plantiga Jr. writes, "*Shalom* means universal flourishing, wholeness, and delight."[179] According to Muehlhoff and Lewis, the Old Testament prophets envisioned *shalom* as "human communities knit together in affirming, flourishing relationships."[180] *Shalom* is peace, yet much more. It is a way of living that glorifies God, the author of peace, by reflecting his character through our practice of tending to the good of human civilization. Civility is essential for the pursuit, protection, and proclamation of shalom. Civility is both an expression of incarnational ministry, and an invitational expression of peace.

So let's say you're still willing to give me that high five. We slap hands, smile in agreement…you've bought in. What now? Christ followers are real people, living an often stress filled life among other stressed-out people.

Add a sluggish economy, aging parents, raising kids, getting through school, and other elements of social life lived in a society that rewards rudeness, and one could understand how a call to civility might just sound like more white noise. Like many of the solutions proposed in section two, the information is solid but complicated and difficult to transfer into busy minds and fast-paced lives.

Christ-followers need the simplexity (something simple but not simplistic, and complex but not complicated) found in a one-word description like shalom- a word that is loaded with explanation but easy to say (simple). A word packed with complex meaning, but simple to remember (memorable). A word that brings to mind a common significance across many experiences (connectable), and a word that carries with it the elements of vision, intention, and means, allowing the user to step through the process of application quickly and efficiently whenever and wherever the opportunity arises (portable). It's a word the reader should be familiar with by now. It's a word related to both the problem and the proposed solutions to the problem. And it's a word that conveys a quality that it seems people want to receive but have a problem expressing.

Have you guessed it? The word is *civil*. Actually, it is an acronym, C.I.V.I.L., but more on that later. Still wondering how it will work? The answer is in the palm of your hand.

Let me give you a hand - your hand.

Bob Goff is a follower of Jesus who people describe as a "one man-tsunami of love, a hurricane of grace."[181] He is also a strong fighter. As an attorney, he aggressively goes after "companies that make crooked skyscrapers or bent buildings…Don't get me wrong, I'm no softy; I can be extremely confrontational when it comes to dirt and two-by-fours."[182] However, Bob fights differently than one might suspect. "I used to think clenched fists would help me fight better, but now I know they make me weaker."[183]

Goff has an unusual practice he requires of his clients when they sit for a deposition. He makes them sit with their hands open and their palms up. Note, the previous sentence says, he "makes them" sit with their palms up. This is a non-negotiable practice for Bob's clients. "I'm very serious about this. In fact I threaten to kick them in the shins if I look down and they don't have their palms up."[184] Goff goes on to explain that when one's palms are up, it is more difficult for them to become defensive or angry. The opposite is accurate, as well. When one clenches their fists, it is much easier to become irritated and aggressive. Goff says, "Something about the hardwiring God gave each of us links the position of our bodies with the position of our hearts. I rarely have a client get frustrated or confused or get tempted to exaggerate or tell a lie when his palms are up."[185]

Goff credits his relationship with Jesus as the motivation for this practice: "Palms up means you have nothing to hide and nothing to gain or lose. Palms up means you are strong enough to be vulnerable, even with your enemies. Even when you have been tremendously wronged. Jesus was palms up, to the end."[186]

Look at your hand. Civility requires followers of Jesus to approach conflict openhanded. The hand will be the image. An open hand with palms up signifies one's openness to be used as an instrument of peace. Now think of the word *civil*. Each finger on the hand will remind us of a different aspect of the conversational process. These memory triggers will help the us recall the various tools explained above. The acrostic below will outline the process, briefly referring to the communication tools each step is connected to.

Are you ready? Palms up, let's go.

C.I.V.I.L. Process

C – Clarity: This first step calls us to clarify the nature of the conflict itself and how we are internally processing the potential conflict. This step poses the question, "What is this about, really?" Such a question allows one to evaluate their own perception and understanding of how the potential conflict is affecting them: (What is this stirring up in me?)

Gaining such clarity allows us to evaluate the nature of and need for further engagement. Does this need to be dealt with right now? Would a delay help or harm the potential resolution? Is this a worthwhile engagement? Is this a hill to die on, or an issue I can overlook? Keep in mind, while convicted and compassionate civility is not the absence of conflict, wisdom dictates that one not go looking for conflict. "A person's wisdom yields patience; it is to one's glory to overlook an offense."[187] Starting the process with clarity allows one to wisely, patiently, and strategically express civility, whether one chooses to further engage the conflict or let it go.

I – Intention: When the conflict is clarified and a decision is reached to further engage, what is the end goal? When a quarterback receives a snap from the center, conflict ensues, but the goal is clear: Reach the end zone. He may have to scramble, improvise, or even take a hard hit, but his intention is certain. For civil conversation, Wilmot and Hocker's shared content goal allows participants to determine what the preferred outcome is. If the conversation is not this deep, at least we can take personal initiative to envision a productive resolution. Intention also references Covey's principle of "beginning with the end in mind."

V – Value: Value is arguably the most important step in the process. The temptation to close the palm and make a fist will be most tangible at this point. It is important here to recall Wilmont and Hocker's relational goal, which determines how one chooses to view the other within the conflict. Because this book is concerned primarily with incivility within the Christian community, value here is based on the relational reality that one is engaged with a brother or sister in Christ, a member of the same Body, a fellow follower of Jesus. As such, while they may be an opponent, they are not the enemy. While they may be irrational, unreasonable, misinformed, or very irritating. Keep in mind that civility does not require that one become close friends with all fellow believers. The fruit of the Spirit is still in season, even if our family quarrel is bitter. Value keeps the hands open and the palms up.

I – Interaction: Interaction pays attention to how the persons involved, and perhaps even the issues discussed, are interdependent on one another. Principles of polarity management and redemptive tension are key in this part of the process. Because some conflicts cannot be resolved because they consist of interdependent opposites (inhaling/exhaling), they are better held in a managed tension. Recalling how to determine the difference is important here: (Does the issue resurface, are there mature and reasonable advocates on both sides, and are the issues interdependent?)

Interaction also reminds us to consider the conversational setting. Is it conducive to practice empathy, presence, and vulnerability when listening to the perspective of another, as explained in Gibb's list above? Remember also that active listening involves interaction in a manner that conveys "cognitive modesty," or reserving the right to be wrong. One can accept the person and affirm their right to express their perspective, while not approving of the perspective or its result.

L – Limits: Christians with a vision, intention, and means to practice compassionate, convicted civility endeavor to extend public politeness, respect, deference, courtesy, kindness, gentleness, and other qualities consistent with the way of Jesus. While conflict is inevitable as long as human beings interact in this world, civility would seek to minimize, resolve, or manage the tensions arising from conflict.

Any healthy interaction, however, contain limits. While some may interpret limits as restrictive measures that infringe on one's freedom, limits can be better defined as measures intended to preserve and protect those engaged, resulting in enhanced freedom. The first humans were placed in Eden with abundant freedom. Once they chose to ignore the one limitation placed by God, their freedom was diminished. Roller coasters limit one's movement, setting one free to experience the ride more than once. Limits are necessary for healthy interaction. This fifth step in the process guides the participant to navigate conflict in a manner that preserves and protects the health of the interaction.

One limitation involves the sort of communication medium to which the conflict will be limited. Will the participants interact face to face, via email, video conferencing, or in some other form? While personal interaction is best, the situation may require communication in a more controlled manner. I once interacted with a fellow Christian who struggled with an explosive temper. In order to converse, the meetings were limited to public, crowded areas like parks, or coffee shops. This aided the gentleman in keeping his cool while we worked through the conflict. Other limitations could include facilitated conversations, mediation, meetings limited by a time frame, or other boundaries that provide the best chance of progress. However, there may come a time when even civility is not enough.

Some conflicts involve issues of such importance that civil responses are difficult. Some behaviors extend beyond the limits of what is tolerable. When bullying brings a person to consider suicide, when people are exploited by evildoers, when sexual predators use their positions within the church to threaten the safety of the innocent, when violent speech and actions are unleashed in a toxic torrent of aggression; setting limits means one concedes there may be times when civility alone is not adequate to deal with one's differences.

Pastor Andy Stanley offers a helpful description. He groups relationships into several circles, two of which are relevant here. One is the circle of influence, where one maintains close ties with those they allow to influence them. The second is the circle of concern.

This circle allows continued connection, but places the relationship outside the realm of influence. The person or group no longer speaks into one's life in a formative or influential way.[188] I refer to this as loving someone from a deliberate distance. In extreme cases, however, the most civil action can be to eliminate contact altogether. This does not imply hatred or un-forgiveness, but recognizes the necessity for such a distance to be put into place. Such limits allow for protection from abusive, oppressive, or even dangerous connections.

Some may question such a decision, but Richard Mouw clarifies that

> Civility is not enough in some situations. But I must repeat: its basic requirements are never canceled. Christians never have a right to simply cast aside kindness and gentleness. We are never justified in engaging in a no-holds-barred crusade against our opponents. Going beyond mere civility does not mean that we become less than civil.[189]

Now that the process has been explained, look at your hand again. The process allows you and me to extend an open hand of civility to others. We can extend our hand in fellowship to another Christian, reach out to meet a stranger, hold the hand of someone hurting, and support someone who is stumbling. The hand can be held up to offer caution to one who is misguided and to grasp one falling away. An open hand is incarnational, sharing the grace of Jesus. An open hand is invitational, calling others to follow the truth that is Jesus. The term *Christian* originally meant "little Christ." That being the case, may our open hands be a prayer that God would make us the kind of people who sound more and look more like Christ.

Questions to Ponder

- What do you think of Bob Goff's "palms up" approach to depositions? Is it something you'd be willing to try? Talk about the results with a group.
- How does an open-handed approach to civil discourse reflect the way of Jesus?
- Talk about the process itself. How easy is it to remember? How does it bring to mind the many different topics, tools, principles, and practical approaches of the book?
- Of the five principles if the C.I.V.I.L. process, which are the most natural for you? Which are more challenging? Why?
- Consider a conflict you recently had, or one you're currently in. How does each aspect of the C.I.V.I.L. process specifically help you establish clarity, intention, value interaction, and limits to that conflict?
- How would you describe this process to another person?
- What was the most important takeaway from this chapter for you?

CONCLUSION

I believe that a convicted, compassionate civility is an expectation placed upon all followers of Jesus Christ. It is the claim of this book that the Christian community's failure to heed these and other demands toward civility, compassion, awareness, and love have worked toward an increasing lack of civility within the Christian community.

In our time together, I've endeavored to address two questions coming from both the church and the wider culture. First, what happened to civility? We have been able to affirm a decline of civility in the fields of business, politics, family, and of particular concern, in the church. The strengths and weaknesses of several proposed solutions were examined, demonstrating a shared sense of need for civility.

Second, where can society learn how to better disagree? The proposal of this book is that the Body of Christ is uniquely positioned, gifted, and commanded to embody a practical and relevant answer to this second question. By embracing a vision for civility, becoming intentional in one's posture toward civility, and adopting practical means to extend civility, the book proposed an embodied response that points to the community of faith as a place and people of grace, wherein civility survives and thrives.

To that end, we have explored principles from a wide spectrum of disciplines including marital therapy, semiotics, polarity management, family systems theory, business management, philosophy, etiquette, art, physics, conflict management, sports, theology, history, and even my daughter's eyeball, and our open hands to demonstrate the need for a process that educates, equips, and empowers Christians to confidently engage in respectful, civil conversations on disputable issues.

It's my sincere hope this book has helped begin a conversation on *why* civility and unity are important, *how* Christians can approach conversations in manner that provides improved solidarity and improved witness to the world, and a simple process helping Christ followers know *what* to do to be the difference in an uncivil world.

As you prepare, practice, and participate in this process, I'd love to hear your story! Email me with your thoughts: kevin@kevinglenn.net

AFTERWORD

Warning: The World is Watching How We
Christians Treat One Another

This is the first Afterword I've ever written for another author. Because Kevin was so convincing in his attempts to persuade me to write it, I didn't have the heart to say "no." So here goes . . .

Recently, someone asked me the following question, "Frank, if I had to summarize your ministry, it would be that Jesus is more than we ever imagined and we can learn to live by His life which is evidenced by treating others the same way we want to be treated. Would you say that this is accurate?" My answer: "Yes, that sums it up well." Most of my blog posts and books are related to these themes, in fact.

Not long ago I wrote a piece for a periodical explaining why I am a Christian, I ended the piece by asking why those who aren't Christians have decided not to follow Jesus (yet, at least). Here's what one person wrote

> I'm not a Christian because of how most of the Christians I've known treat each other. Not loving like their founder taught but just the opposite. I like that your list wasn't apologetic or combative but personal and I respect that. Rare but nice to see.

This harkens back to Gandhi's famous line, "I like your Christ, I do not like your Christians. Your Christians are so unlike your Christ" . . . "If it weren't for Christians, I'd be a Christian."

It's not uncommon for some Christians to throw verbal assaults at one another on Facebook, blogs, Twitter, and other Internet venues. As a result, the world sees people who profess to follow Jesus, the Prince of Peace, fighting, misrepresenting one another, and even "blocking" one another.

"But if you bite and devour one another, take heed that you don't consume one another" (Galatians 5:13).

There once were two cats of Kilkenny
Each thought there was one cat too many
So they fought and they fit
And they scratched and they bit
'Til excepting their nails
And the tips of their tails
Instead of two cats there weren't any.

Civil disagreement and even debate, when done in the spirit of Christ, are healthy and helpful. But when disagreements descend into second-guessing motives, distortions of one another's words, mischaracterizations of one another's views, and personal attacks, then we've moved into the flesh. The net is that the name of Jesus gets tarnished in no small way. So how do we change that?

Kevin's book contributes to this question with elegance, grace, and humor. And I'm glad it exists. Along with Kevin's invitation to civility, here are 7 points to consider the next time you think you have a possible disagreement with another Christian:

1. **Go to them privately and *ask* them what they *meant* by what they said, did, or wrote or what they *allegedly* said, did, or wrote.** Jesus said to go to your brother/sister in private if we have an issue with them. Since we don't want to misrepresent others in public,

going to them directly helps prevent this. And you would want the same treatment if the shoe happened to be on your foot.

About six months ago, I was reading someone's Facebook wall where they quoted a friend of mine who came out with a new book on evangelism. The entire thread was about what my friend *may* have meant or didn't mean. People got angry at one another. Some began blocking others. (These are Christians, mind you.)

Finally, a woman jumped in and said, "Excuse me, but instead of questioning what he may have meant or didn't mean, why don't you just write a message and ask him? He's on Facebook, you know." Her remark arrested everyone and you could smell the embarrassment. Amazingly, no one ever thought to even try to contact my friend and ask. If they had done so in the beginning, the whole issue would have been resolved and the carnage wouldn't have even begun.

2. **When you go to another believer privately, ask them questions. Don't make accusations.**

Again, put yourself in their shoes and ask yourself, "How would I want to be treated if this person was me and I had concerns or possible problems with them?" In my experience, I've found that accusations based on second or third-hand information are usually inaccurate. And they are often rooted in misunderstandings.

One time Jesus made a statement about one of His followers saying, "If I want him to remain alive until I return, what is that to you? You must follow me." Because of this remark, a rumor spread among the disciples that the disciple Jesus was referring to would never die. But Jesus never said that this disciple would not die; he only said, "If I want him to remain alive until I return, what is that to you?" (John 21:22-23)

If Jesus — the perfect Teacher — was misunderstood by those who were in His corner, how much more does it happen with us?

3. **Never, ever, evah, nevah judge the motives or intentions of another human being. To do so is to sin against them and against God.**

You and I cannot read someone else's heart. While it's fine to question someone's judgment, it's wrong to judge their motives. "Love thinks no evil," Paul said in 1 Corinthians 13, but it always believes the best of others. Again, this is covered under Jesus' gold-plated "do unto others" commandment.

4. **Never entertain gossip or slander about another sister or brother in Christ.**

Again, treat others the same way you want them to treat you. Jesus not only commanded this, He said this commandment fulfills the Law and the Prophets (Matt. 7:12). By the way, I've found that many Christians don't know what slander or gossip is (unless it's happening to them). They mistakenly think that if something is true or half-true, it's not gossip or slander. Not so.

Note also that whenever the so-called " truth" is told by someone who is engaging in gossip, it's so distorted that it becomes a lie. Jon Zens' remarkable article on this subject is the best I've ever read. Every Christian should read it: http://frankviola.com/themostignoredsin

5. **Seek peace with all you have. "If it is possible, as far as it depends on you, live at peace with everyone," Paul said in Romans 12:18.**

We aren't going to agree on everything. In fact, I am unaware of any book that exists where all Christians agree with every word or understand every word the same way. That includes the Bible itself. None of us can claim immaculate perception. So we should be open for correction. But how you approach someone is incredibly important. *How we treat one another while we disagree is just as important as the nature of our disagreement.*

6. **Remember that the world is watching how we Christians treat one another and talk about one another.**

This is the thrust of Kevin's book. You can be the greatest evangelist on planet Earth in terms of being able to boldly witness to non-Christians about Jesus. And you can blow the loudest trumpet about mission and discipleship. But if you treat your fellow sisters and brothers in Christ in ways that you would never want to be treated yourself, then you nullify your evangelistic efforts. In addition, how you treat your fellow brothers and sisters is monumentally important to our Lord.

"If Christians cannot extend grace through faithful presence within the body of believers, they will not be able to extend grace to those outside." ~ James Davison Hunter

7. **Remember Jesus' last prayer on earth before He gave His life for us.**

It gives us a peek into what's foremost in His heart. "My prayer is not for them alone. I pray also for those who will believe in me through their message, that all of them may be one, Father, just as you are in me and I am in you. May they also be in us so that the world may believe that you have sent me (John 17:20-21).

In light of these things, may the Lord have mercy on us all . . .
Frank Viola
Author, blogger, speaker, frankviola.org

BIBLIOGRAPHY

Adler, Ronald B., Lawrence B. Rosenfeld, and Russell F. Proctor. *Interplay: The Process of Interpersonal Communication.* New York: Oxford University Press, 2004.

Anderson, Kathy. *Polarity Coaching; Coaching People & Managing Polarities.* Amherst: Human Resource Development Press, 2010.

Arends, Carolyn. "A Both/And Path to Truth." ChristianityToday. com, August 15, 2011. Accessed December 03, 2011. http://www.christianitytoday.com/ct/2011/august/bothpathtruth. html.

"A Bad Day at the Office." *The Covenant Companion* (July 2010): 14-16. Accessed June 2013. http://www.covchurch.org/resources/companion-2010/.

The Baptist Hymnal. Compiled by Wesley L. Forbis. Nashville: Convention Press, 1991. 25.

Beach, Patricia G., and Jennifer Joyce. "Escape From Flatland: Using Polarity Management to Coach Organizational Leaders from a Higher Perspective." *The International Journal of Coaching in Organizations* 7, no. 2 (July 2009): 64-83.

Belcher, Jim. *Deep Church: A Third Way beyond Emerging and Traditional.* Downers Grove: IVP Books, 2009.

_____. "Discovering the Third Way." *Http://blogs. christianbook.com/blogs/academic/2010/05/19/deep-church-an-interview-with-jim-belcher* (blog), May 19, 2010. Accessed December 2, 2011.

Bell, Rob. *Love Wins: A Book About Heaven, Hell, and the Fate of Every Person Who Ever Lived.* New York, NY: Harper One, 2011.

Bellah, Robert N. *Habits of the Heart: Individualism and Commitment in American Life.* Berkeley: Univ. of California Press, 2008.

Bishop, Bill, and Robert G. Cushing. *The Big Sort: Why the Clustering of Like-minded America Is Tearing Us Apart.* Boston: Houghton Mifflin, 2008.

Boyette, Jason. "Thoughts About Rob Bell, John Piper, and Justin Taylor." *O Me of Little Faith,* February 28, 2011. Accessed November 28, 2011. http://blog.beliefnet.com/omeoflittlefaith/.

Burgess, Joseph A. *In Search of Christian Unity: Basic Consensus, Basic Differences.* Minneapolis: Fortress Press, 1991.

Butler, Trent C. *Holman Bible Dictionary.* Nashville: Holman Bible Publishers, 1991.

"Can I Pick Your Brain?" E-mail message to author. February 23, 2013.

Card, Michael. *Matthew: The Gospel of Identity.* Vol. 3. Biblical Imagination Series. Downers Grove: InterVarsity Press, 2013.

Carter, Stephen L. *Civility: Manners, Morals, and the Etiquette of Democracy.* New York: HarperPerennial, 1998.

Chandler, Charles H. "Why Is There Such an Epidemic of Incivility Toward Ministers?" Accessed June 29, 2013. http://www.mtmfoundation.org/Servant/Vol_6_3/v6_3_05.htm.

Cloud, David. "Leonard Sweet Continues Promoting Mystical Heresy." *Reformed Nazarene,* February 7, 2012. http://reformednazarene.wordpress.com/2012/02/07/leonard-sweet-continues-promoting-mystical-heresy/.

Cohen, Daniel H. "For Argument's Sake." TEDx, speech at Colby College, Waterville: February 2013.

Conder, Tim. *The Church in Transition: The Journey of Existing Churches into the Emerging Culture.* Grand Rapids: Zondervan, 2005.

Copan, Paul. *True for You, but Not for Me: Deflating the Slogans That Leave Christians Speechless*. Minneapolis, Bethany House Publishers, 1998.

Covey, Stephen. *The 7 Habits of Highly Effective People*. London: Simon & Schuster, 1999.

Darling, Daniel. "Out of Ur: Friday Five Interview: Mark Demoss." Outofur.com. August 23, 2013. http://www.outofur.com/archives/2013/08/friday_five_int_14.html.

Dombronski, David. "Exposing Contemplative Spirituality." Lighthouse Trails Research Project. Accessed April 04, 2014. http://www.lighthousetrailsresearch.com/leonardsweet.htm.

Downing, Crystal. *Changing Signs of Truth: A Christian Introduction to the Semiotics of Communication*. Downers Grove: IVP Academic, 2012.

Driscoll, Mark. "Speed Round." Lecture, Elephant Room, Harvest Bible Chapel, Chicago, October 10, 2011.

Dudley, Carl, Theresa Zingery, and David Breeden. "Insight Into Congregational Conflict." Faithcommnitiestoday.org. Accessed July 30, 2013. http://faithcommunitiestoday.org/sites/all/themes/factzen4/files/InsightsIntoCongregationalConflict.pdf.

Duhigg, Charles. *The Power of Habit: Why We Do What We Do in Life and Business*. New York: Random House, 2012.

Emerson, Ralph W. "American Civilization." *The Atlantic*, April 1, 1862. http://www.theatlantic.com/magazine/archive/1862/04/american-civilization/306548/?single_page=true.

Fairfax, Gwendolen. "Hello Your Majesty: Rules for Meeting the Royal Family." divinecaroline.com. Accessed July 21, 2013. http://www.divinecaroline.com/life-etc/culture-causes/hello-your-majesty-rules-meeting-royal-family.

Feller, Ben. "Obama Pleads for Civility, Cooperation in Politics." *Denver Post*, 2010. Accessed July 12, 2013. http://www.denverpost.com/popular/ci_14290836.

Finneran, Richard J., ed. *The Collected Works of W.B. Yeats*. 2nd ed. Vol. 1. The Poems. New York: Simon and Schuster, 1996.

Forni, P. M. *Choosing Civility: The Twenty-five Rules of Considerate Conduct*. New York, NY: St. Martin's Griffin, 2003.

_____. *The Civility Solution: What to Do When People Are Rude*. New York: St. Martin's Press, 2008.

Future Church Think Tank 2011: Conversation 02: Adiaphora. Future Church Think Tank 2011. October 29, 2012. https://www.youtube.com/watch?v=YIasfNLyQ1Y&list =PLg6wfFD1rQtvVqr3NL1QIkxdNt_ftE6Sq&index=3.

Gaebelein, Frank E., J. D. Douglas, Merrill C. Tenney, and Richard N. Longenecker. *The Expositor's Bible Commentary: John - Acts: With the New International Version of the Holy Bible*. Grand Rapids: Zondervan Pub. House, 1981.

Gibb, Jack. *The Journal of Communication* 11, no. 3 (September 1961): 141-48. doi:http://www.healthy.net/Health/Article/ Defensive_Communication/2533/1.

Giglio, Louie. Preface. In *Love Does: Discover a Secretly Incredible Life in an Ordinary World*. Nashville: Thomas Nelson, 2012.

Gilbert, Roberta M. *Extraordinary Relationships: A New Way of Thinking about Human Interactions*. Minneapolis: Chronimed Pub., 1992.

Glenn, Kevin D. "On The Edge: Politics in the Church." *Associated Baptist Press* (blog), September 19, 2012. http://www.abpnews.com/blog/uncategorized/on-the-edge-2012-09-19/#.UgAQRJK1Fv8.

Goff, Bob. *Love Does: Discover a Secretly Incredible Life in an Ordinary World*. Nashville: Thomas Nelson, 2012.

Goldman, David. "Internet Has 340 Trillion Trillion Trillion Addresses." CNNMoney. June 06, 2012. http://money.cnn. com/2012/06/06/technology/ipv6/index.htm.

Gottman, John, and Nan Silver. *The Seven Principles for Making Marriage Work*. London: Orion Books, 2007.

_____. *The Marriage Clinic: A Scientifically-based Marital Therapy.* New York: W.W. Norton, 1999.

Greer, Robert. *Mapping Postmodernism: A Survey of Christian Options.* Downers Grove: InterVarsity Press, 2003.

Gregory, Brad S. *The Unintended Reformation: How a Religious Revolution Secularized Society.* Cambridge, Belknap Press of Harvard University Press, 2012.

Guinness, Os. *The Case for Civility: And Why Our Future Depends on It.* New York: HarperOne, 2008.

Hacala, Sara. *Saving Civility: 52 Ways to Tame Rude, Crude, & Attitude for a Polite Planet.* Woodstock: Skylight Paths, 2011.

Hamel, Gary. "Moon Shots for Management." *Harvard Business Review* 87, no. 2 (2009): 91-98.

Huckins, John. "Peacemaking Is a Grassroots Movement | RELEVANT Magazine." RELEVANT Magazine. 2013. Accessed June 29, 2013. http://www.relevantmagazine.com/god/practical-faith/peacemaking-grassroots-movement.

Hunter, James Davison. *To Change the World: The Irony, Tragedy, and Possibility of Christianity in the Late Modern World.* New York: Oxford University Press, 2010.

Hunter, Todd D. *Giving Church Another Chance: Finding New Meaning in Spiritual Practices.* Downers Grove: IVP Books, 2010.

Jacoby, Nicole. "A Crisis of Etiquette." CNN Money. November 29, 1999. http://money.cnn.com/1999/11/29/life/q_manners/.

Johnson, Barry. *Polarity Management: Identifying and Managing Unsolvable Problems.* Amherst, HRD Press, 1992.

Johnson, Steven. *Future Perfect: The Case for Progress in a Networked Age.* New York: Riverhead Books, 2012.

Johnson, Steven. "I Was an Underage Semiotician." *The New York Times*, October 14, 2011. Accessed August 18, 2013. http://www.nytimes.com/2011/10/16/books/review/i-was-an-under-age-semiotician.html?pagewanted=all&_r=0.

Kimball, Dan. *They like Jesus but Not the Church: Insights from Emerging Generations*. Grand Rapids: Zondervan, 2007.

Kinnaman, David, and Aly Hawkins. *You Lost Me: Why Young Christians Are Leaving Church-- and Rethinking Faith*. Grand Rapids: Baker Books, 2011.

———. *Unchristian: What a New Generation Really Thinks about Christianity ... and Why It Matters*. Grand Rapids: Baker Books, 2008.

Kinnaman, Gary. "The Sin of Incivility." *Gary Kinnaman* (blog). Accessed June 21, 2013. http://v2.garykinnaman.com/?p=30.

Lawrenz, Mel. *Whole Church: Leading from Fragmentation to Engagement*. San Francisco: Jossey-Bass, 2009.

Ledbetter, Tammi R. "Rainer: 'Reader Discernment Tags' Scuttled; Efforts to Increase Bible Literacy Prioritized." Southern Baptist Texan / Newsjournal of the Southern Baptists of Texas Convention. February 21, 2008. Accessed December 10, 2011. http://www.texanonline.net/features/rainer-reader-discernment-tags-scuttled-efforts-to-increase-bible-literacy-prioritized.

Leno, Jay, writer. *The Tonight Show with Jay Leno*. NBC. August 7, 2013.

Lewis, C. S. *Mere Christianity*. London: Fount, 1997.

———. *The Weight of Glory*. London: Society for Promoting Christian Knowledge, 1942.

Liu, Eric, and Scott Noppe-Brandon. *Imagination First: Unlocking the Power of Possibility*. San Francisco: Jossey-Bass, 2009.

Lukas, J. Anthony. "Something's Gone Terribly Wrong in New York." Review of *The Closest of Strangers*. *The New York Times*, September 9, 1990. http://www.nytimes.com/1990/09/09/books/something-s-gone-terribly-wrong-in-new-york.html.

Lulofs, Roxane Salyer., and Dudley D. Cahn. *Conflict: From Theory to Action*. Boston: Allyn and Bacon, 2000.

Lulofs, Roxane Salyer., and Dudley D. Cahn. *Conflict: From Theory to Action.* 2nd ed. Boston: Allyn and Bacon, 2000.

Lutzer, Erwin W. *The Doctrines That Divide: A Fresh Look at the Historic Doctrines That Separate Christians.* Grand Rapids: Kregel Publications, 1998.

Lyons, Gabe. *The next Christians: The Good News about the End of Christian America.* New York: Doubleday Religion, 2010.

MacDonald, James. "Unity: Can't We All Just Get Along? vs. Discernment: My Way or the Highway." Lecture, Elephant Room, Harvest Bible Chapel, Chicago, October 10, 2011.

Marty, Martin E. *By Way of Response.* Nashville: Abingdon, 1981.

Maurer, Rick. "Managing Polarities." *Gestalt Review* 6, no. 3 (2002): 209-19.

McConnell, Scott. "LifeWay Research Finds Reasons 18-22 Year Olds Drop Out of Church." Lifeway.com. August 7, 2007. Accessed September 5, 2012. http://www.lifeway.com/ArticleView?storeId=10054.

McKnight, Scot. *The Blue Parakeet: Rethinking How You Read the Bible.* Grand Rapids: Zondervan, 2008.

——————. "What Is the Emerging Church?" Reading, Fall Contemporary Issues Conference, Westminster Theological Seminary, Philadelphia, December 2, 2011.

McLaren, Brian D., and Anthony Campolo. *Adventures in Missing the Point.* Grand Rapids: Zondervan, 2006.

"Meeting The Queen." The British Monarchy. Accessed July 21, 2013. http://www.royal.gov.uk/HMTheQueen/GreetingtheQueen/Overview.aspx.

Milam, Alex C., Christiane Spitzmueller, and Lisa M. Penney. "Investigating Individual Differences among Targets of Workplace Incivility." *Journal of Occupational Health Psychology* 14, no. 1 (2009): 58-69. doi:10.1037/a0012683.

Miller, Donald. *Blue like Jazz: Nonreligious Thoughts on Christian Spirituality.* Nashville: T. Nelson, 2003.

Miller, John Michael. *The Contentious Community: Constructive Conflict in the Church*. Philadelphia: Westminster Press, 1978.

Mohler, Albert. "AlbertMohler.com – A Call for Theological Triage and Christian Maturity." AlbertMohler.com. July 12, 2005. Accessed October 13, 2011. http://www.albertmohler. com/2005/07/12/a-call-for-theological-triage-and-christian-maturity/.

Moore, T. M. *Culture Matters: A Call for Consensus on Christian Cultural Engagement*. Grand Rapids: Brazos Press, 2007.

Mouw, Richard J. *Uncommon Decency: Christian Civility in an Uncivil World*. Downers Grove: InterVarsity Press, 2010.

Muehlhoff, Tim, and Todd Vernon Lewis. *Authentic Communication: Christian Speech Engaging Culture*. Downers Grove: IVP Academic, 2010.

Ogden, C. K., and I. A. Richards. *The Meaning of Meaning*. London: Kegan Paul, 1923.

Oldenburg, Ray. *The Great Good Place: Cafés, Coffee Shops, Community Centers, Beauty Parlors, General Stores, Bars, Hangouts, and How They Get You through the Day*. New York: Paragon House, 1989.

Olson, Roger E. "Why Can't Southern Baptists Just Get along." *Roger E. Olson* (blog), July 8, 2012. Accessed July 30, 2013. http://www.patheos.com/blogs/rogereolson/2012/07/why-cant-southern-baptists-just-get-along/.

Oswald, Roy M., and Barry Allan Johnson. *Managing Polarities in Congregations: Eight Keys for Thriving Faith Communities*. Herndon: Alban Institute, 2010.

Page, Scott E. *The Difference: How the Power of Diversity Creates Better Groups, Firms, Schools, and Societies*. Princeton: Princeton University Press, 2007.

Parham, Robert. "How Churches Can Help Our Nation Embrace Civility." Ethicsdaily.com. November 11, 2012. http://www.

ethicsdaily.com/how-churches-can-help-our-nation-embrace-civility-cms-20184.

Pearson, Christine, and Christine Porath. "The Cost of Bad Behavior: How Incivility Is Damaging The Workplace And What To Do About It." The Cost of Bad Behavior: How Incivility Is Damaging The Workplace And What To Do About It. July 9, 2009. Accessed June 12, 2013. http://www.thecostofbadbehavior.com/home.html.

Pearson, Christine M., and Christine Lynne. Porath. *The Cost of Bad Behavior: How Incivility Is Damaging Your Business and What to Do about It.* New York: Portfolio, 2009.

Peirce, Charles S. "Logic as Semiotic: The Theory of Signs." In *Philosophical Writings of Peirce,*, edited by Justus Buchler. New York: Dover Publications, 1955.

_____. *Collected Papers of Charles Sanders Peirce.* Edited by Arthur W. Burks. Bristol: Thoemmes Press, 1998.

Pippin, Robert B. *The Persistence of Subjectivity: On the Kantian Aftermath.* Cambridge, UK: Cambridge University Press, 2005.

Plantiga, Cornelius, Jr. *Not the Way It;s Supposed to Be: A Breviary of Sin.* Grand Rapids: Eerdman's, 1995.

Platt, David. "Poverty Theology vs. Prosperity Theology." Lecture, Elephant Room Conference, Harvest Bible Chapel, Chicago, October 10, 2011.

Pohl, Christine D. *Making Room: Recovering Hospitality as a Christian Tradition.* Grand Rapids: W.B. Eerdmans, 1999.

Polanyi, Michael. *Personal Knowledge; towards a Post-critical Philosophy.* Chicago: University of Chicago Press, 1958.

Pratt, Richard L., Jr. "Pictures, Windows, and Mirrors in Old Testament Exegesis." *Westminster Theological Journal* 45, no. 1 (Spring 1983): 56-67.

Putnam, Robert D. *Bowling Alone: The Collapse and Revival of American Community.* New York: Simon & Schuster, 2000.

Rainer, Thom S., and Sam S. Rainer. *Essential Church?: Reclaiming a Generation of Dropouts*. Nashville: B & H Books, 2008.

Richardson, John. "Open versus Closed Ended Questions." UCLA Department of Information Studies. November 24, 2008. Accessed November 11, 2011. http://polaris.gseis.ucla.edu/jrichardson/dis220/openclosed.htm.

Richardson, Ronald W. *Creating a Healthier Church: Family Systems Theory, Leadership, and Congregational Life*. Minneapolis: Fortress Press, 1996.

Robinson, Kerry. "Faith's Response to Incivility." *On Faith Panelists Blog:* (web log), September 19, 2009. Accessed June 29, 2013. http://newsweek.washingtonpost.com/onfaith/panelists/kerry_robinson/2009/09/faiths_response_to_incivility.html.

Schulz, Kathryn. *Being Wrong: Adventures in the Margin of Error*. New York: Ecco, 2010.

Shelley, Marshall. "Electronic Warfare." *Christianity Today*, Summer 2013. Accessed August 6, 2013. http://www.christianitytoday.com/le/2013/summer/electronic-warfare.html?paging=off.

Simon, Roger. "Those Dumber Than You." *Politico*, November 1, 2012. Accessed June 6, 2013. http://www.politico.com/news/stories/1112/83345_Page2.html.

Slaughter, Michael, Charles E. Gutenson, and Robert P. Jones. *Hijacked: Responding to the Partisan Church Divide*. Nashville: Abingdon Press, 2012.

Solomonson, Sonia C. "A Bad Day at the Office." *The Covenant Companion*, July 2010, 14-16. Accessed June 26, 2013. http://www.covchurch.org/resources/files/2010/01/7.2010.July-Civility.pdf.

Stanley, Andy. Lecture, Drive 2010, Northpoint Community Church, Atlanta, October 2010.

_____. "The Opposable Leader." Speech, Drive Conference 2010, Northpoint Community Church, Atlanta, November 16, 2011.

_____. "The Power of Friendship." Speech, North Point Community Church, Alpharetta, March 2007.

Stanton, Graham. *The Gospels and Jesus.* Oxford: Oxford University Press, 1989.

Steinmetz, Katy. "Elections Leave Congress Divided, Further from Compromise." *Time Swampland,* 2012. http://swampland.time.com/2012/11/07/will-the-new-congress-pump-the-brakes-on-partisanship/.

Stott, John R. W. *Evangelical Truth: A Personal Plea for Unity, Integrity, and Faithfulness.* Downers Grove: InterVarsity Press, 2005.

Stroh, Peter, and Wayne Miller. "Learning to Thrive on Paradox." *Training and Development,* September 1994, 28-39.

"Suggested Edits to Politics Piece." E-mail message to author. September 16, 2012.

Sweeney, John. *Return to Civility: A Speed of Laughter Project.* Minneapolis, MN: Aerialist, 2007.

_____. "Return To Civility." Return To Civility. January 2008. http://return-to-civility.com/.

Sweet, Leonard. Comment on "Conversation 02: Adiphora." *George Fox Evangelical Seminary* (video blog), July 11, 2011. Accessed November 2, 2011. http://vimeo.com/gfes.

_____. *So Beautiful: Divine Design for Life and the Church: Missional, Relational, Incarnational.* Colorado Springs: David C. Cook, 2009.

_____. "Relational Objectivity." Lecture, Doctor of Ministry Cohort Advance, George Fox Evangelical Seminary, Portland, August 24, 2011.

Swindoll, Charles R. "The Gymnasium of the Soul." Insight for Living. August 2008. http://www.insightforliving.ca/insights/humility/gymnasium-soul.html.

Teinowitz, Ira. "Republicans Ban CNN, NBC From Hosting Debates Because of Hillary Clinton Projects." *TheWrap.com,* Accessed August 16, 2013. http://www.thewrap.com/tv/

article/republicans-wont-let-cnn-nbc-host-debates-because-clinton-projects-111301.

Thomas, Kenneth Wayne, and Ralph H. Kilmann. *Thomas-Kilmann Conflict Mode Instrument*. Tuxedo: XICOM, 1974.

Tippet, Krista. "About On Being." On Being. Accessed July 31, 2013. http://www.onbeing.org.

Viola, Frank. "Hearing One Side of the Story." *Frank Viola-The Deeper Journey* (web log), December 28, 2012. http://www.patheos.com/blogs/frankviola/hearingonesideofastory/.

_____. "Warning: The World Is Watching How We Christians Treat One Another." *Beyond Evangelical* (blog), January 14, 2013. http://frankviola.org/2013/01/14/warning/.

W, W. "Incivility in the Church." Words from WW Blog. February 22, 2013. Accessed June 29, 2013. http://wordsfromww.com/2013/02/22/incivility-in-the-church/.

Walker, Andrew. "CBF-Yesterday's Moderates Are Today's Conservatives." *Baptist Press*, May 1, 2012. http://www.bpnews.net/BPFirstPerson.asp?ID=37735.

_____. "Gay Issue Major Theme of CBF-sponsored Conf. - Baptist Press. April 23, 2012. http://bpnews.net/BPnews.asp?ID=37666.

Weckerle, Andrea. *Civility in the Digital Age: How Companies and People Can Triumph over Haters, Trolls, Bullies, and Other Jerks*. Indianapolis: Que, 2013.

Whorthen, Molly. "The Reformer." *Christianity Today*, October 1, 2010, 18-21. http://www.christianitytoday.com/ct/2010/october/3.18.html?paging=off.

Willard, Dallas. *Renovation of the Heart: Putting on the Character of Christ*. Colorado Springs: NavPress, 2002.

Wilmot, William W., and Joyce L. Hocker. *Interpersonal Conflict*. 8th ed. Boston: McGraw-Hill, 2007.

Wilson, Bill. "The Both/And Life of Faith." *Associated Baptist Press*, November 20, 2012. http://www.abpnews.com/opinion/item/7988-the-both-and-life-of-faith#.UgG4lJK1Fv9.

_____. "The Conflict Pandemic." *ABP News*. November 2, 2012. http://www.abpnews.com/opinion/item/7942-the-conflict-pandemic.

Witherington, Ben. *Conflict and Community in Corinth: A Socio-rhetorical Commentary on 1 and 2 Corinthians*. Grand Rapids: W.B. Eerdmans, 1995.

Wood, Shawn. "The Christian Cannibal Culture." *Shawnwoodwrites.com* (web log), January 10, 2013. http://shawnwoodwrites.com/blog/the-christian-canibal-culture/.

Woodbridge, John D. "Culture War Casualties: How Warfare Rhetoric Is Hurting the Work of the Church." *Christianity Today*, March 6, 1995, 21-26.

ENDNOTES

1   John Sweeney, "Return to Civility," Return to Civility, January 2008, http://return-to-civility.com/.

2   Sara Hacala, *Saving Civility: 52 Ways to Tame Rude, Crude, & Attitude for a Polite Planet* (Woodstock, VT: Skylight Paths, 2011), 3.

3   P.M. Forni, *The Civility Solution: What to Do When People Are Rude* (New York: St.Martin's Press, 2008), 9.

4   Gwendolen Fairfax, "Hello Your Majesty: Rules for Meeting the Royal Family." Www.divinecaroline.com, accessed July 21, 2013, http://www.divinecaroline.com/life-etc/culture-causes/hello-your-majesty-rules-meeting-royal-family.

5   "Meeting The Queen," The British Monarchy, accessed July 21, 2013, http://www.royal.gov.uk/HMTheQueen/GreetingtheQueen/Overview.aspx.

6   P. M. Forni, *Choosing Civility the Twenty-five Rules of Considerate Conduct* (New York, NY: St. Martin's Griffin, 2003), 10.

7   Stephen L. Carter, *Civility: Manners, Morals, and the Etiquette of Democracy* (New York: Harper Perennial, 1998), 14.

8   Forni, *Choosing Civility*, 10.

9   Carter, *Civility*, 16

10 Carter, Civility, 11.

11 Ibid., 14.

12 Hacala, *Saving Civility*, 8.

13 Richard J. Mouw, *Uncommon Decency: Christian Civility in an Uncivil World* (Downers Grove: InterVarsity Press, 2010), 14.

14 Mouw, *Uncommon Decency*, 14.

15 Mouw, *Uncommon Decency*, 11.

16 Ira Teinowitz, "Republicans Ban CNN, NBC From Hosting Debates Because of Hillary Clinton Projects," *TheWrap.com*, August 16, 2013, http://www.thewrap.com/tv/article/republicans-wont-let-cnn-nbc-host-debates-because-clinton-projects-111301.

17 Jay Leno, writer, *The Tonight Show with Jay Leno*, NBC, August 7, 2013.

18 Kerry Robinson, "Faith's Response to Incivility," *On Faith Panelists Blog:* (web log), September 19, 2009, summary, accessed June 29,

2013, http://newsweek.washingtonpost.com/onfaith/panelists/kerry_robinson/2009/09/faiths_response_to_incivility.html.

[19] Gary Kinnaman, "The Sin of Incivility," *Gary Kinnaman* (blog), accessed June 21, 2013, http://v2.garykinnaman.com/?p=30.

[20] Ben Feller, "Obama Pleads for Civility, Cooperation in Politics," *Denver Post*, 2010, accessed July 12, 2013, http://www.denverpost.com/popular/ci_14290836.

[21] Katy Steinmetz, "Elections Leave Congress Divided, Further from Compromise," *Time Swampland*, 2012, summary, http://swampland.time.com/2012/11/07/will-the-new-congress-pump-the brakes-on-partisanship/.

[22] Robert Parham, "How Churches Can Help Our Nation Embrace Civility," Ethicsdaily.com, November 11, 2012, introduction, http://www.ethicsdaily.com/how-churches-can-help-our-nation-embrace-civility-cms-20184.

[23] Roger Simon, "Those Dumber Than You," Politico, November 1, 2012, accessed June 6, 2013, http://www.politico.com/news/stories/1112/83345_Page2.html

[24] Kinnaman, "The Sin of Incivility."

[25] Sonia C. Solomonson, "A Bad Day at the Office," *The Covenant Companion*, July 2010, 15, accessed June 26, 2013, http://www.covchurch.org/resources/files/2010/01/7.2010.July-Civility.pdf.

[26] Christine M. Pearson and Christine Lynne Porath, *The Cost of Bad Behavior: How Incivility Is Damaging Your Business and What to Do about It* (New York: Portfolio, 2009), 4.

[27] John Mordechai Gottman, *The Marriage Clinic: a Scientifically-based Marital Therapy* (New York: W.W. Norton, 1999), 96.

[28] Gottman, *The Marriage Clinic.*, 235.

[29] Ibid.

[30] Ibid.

[31] Gottman., The Marriage Clinic,2.

[32] Ibid., 27.

[33] Ibid., 29

[34] Ibid., 36

[35] Roberta M. Gilbert, *Extraordinary Relationships: A New Way of Thinking about Human Interactions* (Minneapolis: Chronimed Pub., 1992), 55.

[36] Ronald W. Richardson, *Creating a Healthier Church: Family Systems Theory, Leadership, and Congregational Life* (Minneapolis: Fortress Press, 1996), 114

37 Robert B. Pippin, *The Persistence of Subjectivity: On the Kantian Aftermath* (Cambridge: Cambridge University Press, 2005), 227.

38 Daniel Darling, "Out of Ur: Friday Five Interview: Mark Demoss," Outofur.com, August 23, 2013, http://www.outofur.com/archives/2013/08/friday_five_int_14.html.

39 Bill Wilson, "The Conflict Pandemic," ABP News, November 2, 2012, http://www.abpnews.com/opinion/item/7942-the-conflict-pandemic.

40 Wilson, "The Conflict Pandemic"

41 Carl Dudley, Theresa Zingery, and David Breeden, "Insight Into Congregational Conflict," Faithcommnitiestoday.org, pg.1, accessed July 30, 2013, http://faithcommunitiestoday.org/sites/all/themes/factzen4/files/InsightsIntoCongregationalConflict.pdf.

42 Kinnaman, "The Sin of Incivility,".

43 Shawn Wood, "The Christian Cannibal Culture," *Shawnwoodwrites.com* (web log), January 10, 2013, http://shawnwoodwrites.com/blog/the-christian-canibal-culture/.

44 Roger E. Olson, "Why Can't Southern Baptists Just Get along," *Roger E. Olson* (blog), July 8, 2012, accessed July 30, 2013, http://www.patheos.com/blogs/rogereolson/2012/07/why-cant-southern-baptists-just-get-along/.

45 Charles H. Chandler, "Why Is There Such an Epidemic of Incivility Toward Ministers?", accessed June 29, 2013, http://www.mtmfoundation.org/Servant/Vol_6_3/v6_3_05.htm.

46 Kerry Robinson, "Faith's Response to Incivility," *On Faith Panelists Blog:* (web log), September 19, 2009, accessed June 29, 2013, http://newsweek.washingtonpost.com/onfaith/panelists/kerry_robinson/2009/09/faiths_response_to_incivility.html

47 Mouw, *Uncommon Decency,* 12.

48 Mel Lawrenz, *Whole Church: Leading from Fragmentation to Engagement* (San Francisco, CA: Jossey-Bass, 2009), 5.

49 Hacala, *Saving Civility,* 3.

50 Ibid., 4.

51 Ibid.,7.

52 Ibid.,7.

53 Forni, *Choosing Civility,* 25

54 Pearson and Porath, *The Cost of Bad Behavior,* 123.

55 Ibid., 8.

56 Christine Pearson and Christine Porath, *The Cost of Bad Behavior: How Incivility Is Damaging The Workplace And What To Do About It,* July 9, 2009, accessed June 12, 2013, http://www.thecostofbadbehavior.com/

home.html.

57   Pearson and Porath, *The Cost of Bad Behavior*, 138.

58   Ibid., 155

59   Ibid., 163.

60   Pearson and Porath, *The Cost of Bad Behavior,* 179.

61   Alex C. Milam, Christiane Spitzmueller, and Lisa M. Penney, "Investigating Individual Differences among Targets of Workplace Incivility.," *Journal of Occupational Health Psychology* 14, no. 1 (2009): 63-65, doi:10.1037/a0012683.

62   Charles Duhigg, *The Power of Habit: Why We Do What We Do in Life and Business* (New York: Random House, 2012), 118-119.

63   Ibid., 120.

64   Ben Witherington, *Conflict and Community in Corinth: A Socio-rhetorical Commentary on 1 and 2 Corinthians* (Grand Rapids, MI: W.B. Eerdmans, 1995), 258.

65   Solomonson, "A Bad Day at the Office,"

66   Crystal Downing, *Changing Signs of Truth: A Christian Introduction to the Semiotics of Communication* (Downers Grove, IL: IVP Academic, 2012), 105.

67   Downing, *Changing Signs of Truth,* 109.

68   Ibid., 110.

69   Ogden and Richards, 282.

70   Downing, 199.

71   Downing, *Changing Signs of Truth,* 110.

72   Charles Sanders Peirce, "Logic as Semiotic: The Theory of Signs," in *Philosophical Writings of Peirce,*, ed. Justus Buchler (New York: Dover Publications, 1955), 99.

73   Charles Sanders Peirce, *Collected Papers of Charles Sanders Peirce.*, ed. Arthur W. Burks (Bristol: Thoemmes Press, 1998), 136.

74   Leonard I. Sweet, *So Beautiful: Divine Design for Life and the Church: Missional, Relational, Incarnational* (Colorado Springs, CO: David C. Cook, 2009), 35.

75   Barry Johnson, *Polarity Management: Identifying and Managing Unsolvable Problems* (Amherst, Mass: HRD Press, 1992), xvii.

76   Johnson, *Polarity Management.*, 209

77   Ibid., xviii.

78   Roy M. Oswald and Barry Allan Johnson, *Managing Polarities in Congregations: Eight Keys for Thriving Faith Communities* (Herndon, VA: Alban Institute, 2010), 11.

79 Kathy Anderson, *Polarity Coaching Coaching People & Managing Polarities*. (Amherst: Human Resource Development Pr, 2010), xii.

80 Sweet, *So Beautiful*, 45.

81 Ibid., 46.

82 Andy Stanley (lecture, Drive 2010, Northpoint Community Church, Atlanta, October 2010).

83 Oswald and Johnson, *Managing Polarities in Congregations*, 1.

84 Bill Wilson, "The both/and life of faith," *Associated Baptist Press*, November 20, 2012, http://www.abpnews.com/opinion/item/7988-the-both-and-life-of-faith#.UgG4lJK1Fv9.

85 Carolyn Arends, "A Both/And Path to Truth | Christianity Today | A Magazine of Evangelical Conviction," ChristianityToday.com | Magazines, News, Church Leadership & Bible Study, August 15, 2011, accessed December 03, 2011, http://www.christianitytoday.com/ct/2011/august/bothpathtruth.html.

86 1 Corinthians 9:24

87 David Goldman, "Internet Has 340 Trillion Trillion Trillion Addresses," CNNMoney, June 06, 2012, http://money.cnn.com/2012/06/06/technology/ipv6/index.htm.

88 Andrea Weckerle, *Civility in the Digital Age: How Companies and People Can Triumph over Haters, Trolls, Bullies, and Other Jerks* (Indianapolis, IN: Que, 2013), 6.

89 Marshall Shelley, "Electronic Warfare," *Christianity Today*, Summer 2013, accessed August 6, 2013, http://www.christianitytoday.com/le/2013/summer/electronic-warfare.html?paging=off.

90 David Cloud, "Reformed Nazarene," Reformed Nazarene, February 7, 2012, section goes here, accessed April 04, 2014, http://reformednazarene.wordpress.com/2012/02/07/leonard-sweet-continues-promoting-mystical-heresy/.

91 Weckerle, *Civility in the Digital Age,* 88.

92 Ibid, 91.

93 Weckerle, *Civility in the Digital Age,* 14.

94 Ibid, 24.

95 Carter, *Civility,* xii.

96 Forni, *Choosing Civility*, 9.

97 Ibid, 14.

98 Ibid, 27.

99 P. M. Forni, *The Civility Solution: What to Do When People Are Rude* (New York: St. Martin's Press, 2008), 6.

100   Jim Belcher, *Deep Church: A Third Way beyond Emerging and Traditional* (Downers Grove, IL: IVP Books, 2009), 54.

101   John R. W. Stott, *Evangelical Truth: A Personal Plea for Unity, Integrity, and Faithfulness* (Downers Grove, IL: InterVarsity Press, 2005), 116.

102   John Michael Miller, *The Contentious Community: Constructive Conflict in the Church* (Philadelphia: Westminster Press, 1978), 16.

103   John D. Woodbridge, "Culture War Casualties: How Warfare Rhetoric Is Hurting the Work of the Church," *Christianity Today*, March 6, 1995, 22.

104   Ibid, 22.

105   Tim Muehlhoff and Todd Vernon Lewis, Authentic Communication: Christian Speech Engaging Culture (Downers Grove, IL: IVP Academic, 2010). *54*.

106   Molly Whorthen, "The Reformer," *Christianity Today*, October 1, 2010, 18, http://www.christianitytoday.com/ct/2010/october/3.18.html?paging=off.

107   Ibid, 19.

108   Ibid.

109   Andrew Walker, "CBF-Yesterday's Moderates Are Today's Conservatives," *Baptist Press*, May 1, 2012, http://www.bpnews.net/BPFirstPerson.asp?ID=37735.

110   Andrew Walker, "Gay Issue Major Theme of CBF-sponsored Conf. - News with a Christian Perspective," Baptist Press, April 23, 2012, http://bpnews.net/BPnews.asp?ID=37666.

111   Scot McKnight, "What Is the Emerging Church?" (reading, Fall Contemporary Issues Conference, Westminster Theological Seminary, Philadelphia, December 2, 2011).

112   Kinnaman, "The Sin of Incivility"

113   McKnight, "What Is The Emerging Church?"

114   Os Guinness, *The Case for Civility: And Why Our Future Depends on It* (New York: HarperOne, 2008), 19.

115   Hacala, 31.

116   Gabe Lyons, *The next Christians: The Good News about the End of Christian America* (New York: Doubleday Religion, 2010), 173.

117   Forni, *Choosing Civility,*27.

118   Dallas Willard, *Renovation of the Heart: Putting on the Character of Christ* (Colorado Springs, CO: NavPress, 2002), 85.

119   John13:35

120   Frank Viola, "Warning: The World Is Watching How We Christians

Treat One Another," *Beyond Evangelical* (web log), January 14, 2013, http://frankviola.org/2013/01/14/warning/.

121 Muehlhoff and Lewis, *Authentic Communication*, 104.

122 Mel Lawrenz, *Whole Church: Leading from Fragmentation to Engagement* (San Francisco: Jossey-Bass, 2009), 12.

123 Ibid, 21.

124 Muehlhoff and Lewis, *Authentic Communication*, 104.

125 In this sense, practice does not make perfect, but it allows for improvement and reveals the space for further improvement. It is an effort of repetition where the end is not completion, but continued execution much like attorneys "practice" law or doctors "practice" medicine. "Practicing" Christians "practice" their faith.

126 A concise exploration of Jesus' conflict with and between his disciples as well as the religious leaders of his day is offered in Graham Stanton, *The Gospels and Jesus* (Oxford [England: Oxford University Press, 1989), 44-47.

127 Galatians 2:8-15

128 Acts 15:1-35

129 1 Corinthians 1:10-17, Philippians 4:1-3

130 Ralph W. Emerson, "American Civilization," *The Atlantic*, April 1, 1862, 2, http://www.theatlantic.com/magazine/archive/1862/04/american-civilization/306548/?single_page=true.

131 Emerson, "American Civilization."

132 Ibid.

133 J. Anthony Lukas, "Something's Gone Terribly Wrong in New York," review of *The Closest of Strangers*, *The New York Times*, September 9, 1990, http://www.nytimes.com/1990/09/09/books/something-s-gone-terribly-wrong-in-new-york.html.

134 Richard J. Finneran, ed., *The Collected Works of W.B. Yeats*, 2nd ed., vol. 1, The Poems (New York: Simon and Schuster, 1996), 182.

135 Martin E. Marty, *By Way of Response* (Nashville: Abingdon, 1981), 81.

136 Mouw, *Uncommon Decency*, 14.

137 Paul Copan, *True for You, but Not for Me: Deflating the Slogans That Leave Christians Speechless* (Minneapolis: Bethany House Publishers, 1998), 32.

138 Michael Card, *Matthew: The Gospel of Identity*, vol. 3, Biblical Imagination Series (Downers Grove: InterVarsity Press, 2013), 68.

139 Mouw, *Uncommon Decency*, 24.

140 Mouw, *Uncommon Decency*, 19.

141   Leonard Sweet, "Relational Objectivity" (lecture, Doctor of Ministry Cohort Advance, George Fox Evangelical Seminary, Portland, August 24, 2011).

142   Christine D. Pohl, *Making Room: Recovering Hospitality as a Christian Tradition* (Grand Rapids: W.B. Eerdmans, 1999), 31.

143   Trent C. Butler, *Holman Bible Dictionary* (Nashville: Holman Bible Publishers, 1991), 941.

144   Aurelius Augustinus, *City of God*, trans. Gill Evans and Henry Bettenson (London: Penguin, 2003), 460.

145   Kathryn Schulz, *Being Wrong: Adventures in the Margin of Error* (New York: Ecco, 2010), pp. 5-6.

146   Such an approach was emphasized at "The Elephant Room," a conference organized to hold direct, but civil conversations between pastors of differing theological, philosophical, and methodological approaches to ministry. Participants were asked about a series of issues and were instructed to answer whether they believed such issues were "State" (areas of disagreement, but not worthy of going to war) or "National" (boundaries of orthodox identity that must be defended) issues. Among the issues described as "National" were evolution, inerrancy of scripture, and belief in a literal hell. James MacDonald, " Unity: Why can't we just all get along? vs. Discernment: My way or the highway. ", (lecture, Elephant Room, Harvest Bible Chapel, Chicago, October 10, 2011).

147   David Platt, "Poverty Theology vs. Prosperity Theology" (lecture, Elephant Room Conference, Harvest Bible Chapel, Chicago, October 10, 2011).

148   Carolyn Arends, "A Both/And Path to Truth | Christianity Today | A Magazine of Evangelical Conviction," ChristianityToday.com | Magazines, News, Church Leadership & Bible Study, August 15, 2011.

149   Frederick W. Faber. "There's A Wideness in God's Mercy*"in The Baptist Hymnal,* Comp. Wesley L. Forbis (Nashville, TN: Convention Press, 1991), 25

150   C. S. Lewis, *Mere Christianity* (London: Fount, 1997), vi, xi.

151   Jim Belcher, "Discovering the Third Way," interview, *Http://blogs. christianbook.com/blogs/academic/2010/05/19/deep-church-an-interview-with-jim-belcher* (web log), May 19, 2010, accessed December 2, 2011.

152   Albert Mohler, "AlbertMohler.com – A Call for Theological Triage and Christian Maturity," AlbertMohler.com, July 12, 2005, accessed October 13, 2011, http://www.albertmohler. com/2005/07/12/a-call-for-theological-triage-and-christian-maturity/.

153 Ibid.

154 *Future Church Think Tank 2011: Conversation 02: Adiaphora*, prod. Leonard I. Sweet, perf. 2011 Future Church Think Tank, Future Church Think Tank 2011, October 29, 2012, https://www.youtube.com/watch?v=YIasfNLyQ1Y&list=PLg6wfFD1rQtvVqr3NL1QIkxdNt_ftE6Sq&index=3.

155 Robert Greer, *Mapping Postmodernism: A Survey of Christian Options* (Downers Grove, IL: InterVarsity Press, 2003), 174.

156 Steven Johnson, *Future Perfect: The Case for Progress in a Networked Age* (New York: Riverhead Books, 2012), 97.

157 "If two collections of problem solvers contain problem solvers of equal individual ability, and if those problem solvers in the first collection are homogenous and those in the second collection are diverse, that is, they have some differences in their local optima, then the collection of diverse problem solvers, on average, outperforms the collection of homogenous problem solvers." Scott E. Page, *The Difference: How the Power of Diversity Creates Better Groups, Firms, Schools, and Societies* (Princeton: Princeton University Press, 2007), 157.

158 Frank E. Gaebelein et al., *The Expositor's Bible Commentary: John - Acts: With the New International Version of the Holy Bible* (Grand Rapids: Zondervan Pub. House, 1981), 142.

159 Mouw, *Uncommon Decency*, 13.

160 Kinnaman, "The Sin of Incivility."

161 Muehlhoff and Lewis, *Authentic Communication*, 102.

162 James Davison Hunter, *To Change the World: The Irony, Tragedy, and Possibility of Christianity in the Late Modern World* (New York: Oxford University Press, 2010), 244.

163 Muehlhoff and Lewis, *Authentic Communication*, 30.

164 Mouw, *Uncommon Decency*, 38.

165 1 Timothy 4:7-8

166 Charles R. Swindoll, "The Gymnasium of the Soul," Insight for Living, August 2008, section goes here, http://www.insightforliving.ca/insights/humility/gymnasium-soul.html

167 Leonard Sweet's upcoming book is dedicated entirely to the notion of practice and play; two concepts he has frequently "played with" throughout the author's academic program.

168 *Third space*, is a term used to refer to social surroundings different from home (first space) and work (second place). In his book *The Great Good Place*, Ray Oldenburg suggests that third spaces are important for

building civil community, civil engagement, and establishing feelings of a sense of place. Ray Oldenburg, *The Great Good Place: Cafés, Coffee Shops, Community Centers, Beauty Parlors, General Stores, Bars, Hangouts, and How They Get You through the Day* (New York: Paragon House, 1989).

169   William W. Wilmot and Joyce L. Hocker, *Interpersonal Conflict*, 8th ed. (Boston: McGraw-Hill, 2007). 71-83

170   Stephen Covey, *The 7 Habits of Highly Effective People.* (London: Simon & Schuster, 1999), 97.

171   Gary Kinnaman, "The Sin of Incivility."

172   Proverbs 15:1

173   Jack Gibb, *The Journal of Communication* 11, no. 3 (September 1961): 142, doi:http://www.healthy.net/Health/Article/Defensive_Communication/2533/1.

174   Jim Belcher, "Discovering the Third Way," interview, *Http://blogs.christianbook.com/blogs/academic/2010/05/19/deep-church-an-interview-with-jim-belcher* (web log), May 19, 2010, accessed December 2, 2011.

175   Ronald B. Adler, Lawrence B. Rosenfeld, and Russell F. Proctor, *Interplay: The Process of Interpersonal Communication* (New York: Oxford University Press, 2004), 303.

176   Mouw, *Uncommon Decency*, 76.

177   Richard L. Pratt, Jr., "Pictures, Windows, and Mirrors in Old Testament Exegesis," *Westminster Theological Journal* 45, no. 1 (Spring 1983). 56-67.

178   Muehlhoff and Lewis, *Authentic Communication*, 44.

179   Cornelius Plantiga, Jr., *Not the Way It's Supposed to Be: A Breviary of Sin* (Grand Rapids: Eerdmans, 1995), 10.

180   Muehlhoff and Lewis, *Authentic Communication*, 116.

181   Louie Giglio, preface, in *Love Does: Discover a Secretly Incredible Life in an Ordinary World* (Nashville: Thomas Nelson, 2012).

182   Bob Goff, *Love Does: Discover a Secretly Incredible Life in an Ordinary World* (Nashville: Thomas Nelson, 2012), 203.

183   Ibid.

184   Ibid., 204.

185   Ibid., 205.

186   Goff, *Love Does*, 205

187   Proverbs 19:11

188   Andy Stanley, "The Power of Friendship" (speech, North Point Community Church, Alpharetta, March 2007).

189   Mouw, *Uncommon Decency*, 147.

Made in the USA
Coppell, TX
27 June 2021